SpringerBriefs in Quantitati

SpringerBriefs present concise summaries of cutting-edge research and practical applications across a wide spectrum of fields. Featuring compact volumes of 50 to 125 pages, the series covers a range of content from professional to academic. Briefs are characterized by fast, global electronic dissemination, standard publishing contracts, standardized manuscript preparation and formatting guidelines, and expedited production schedules.

Typical topics might include:

- A timely report of state-of-the art techniques
- A bridge between new research results, as published in journal articles, and a contextual literature review
- A snapshot of a hot or emerging topic
- An in-depth case study

SpringerBriefs in Quantitative Finance showcase topics of current relevance in the field of mathematical finance in a compact format. Published titles will feature both academic-inspired work and more practitioner-oriented material, with a special focus on the application of recent mathematical techniques to finance, including areas such as derivatives pricing and financial engineering, risk measures and risk allocation, risk management and portfolio optimization, computational methods, and statistical modelling of financial data.

More information about this series at http://www.springer.com/series/8784

Ulrich Bindseil · Alessio Fotia

Introduction to Central Banking

 Springer

Ulrich Bindseil
Institute of Economics and Law
Macroeconomics
Technical University Berlin
Berlin, Germany

Market Infrastructures and Payments
European Central Bank
Frankfurt, Germany

Alessio Fotia
School of Business and Economics
Freie Universität Berlin
Berlin, Germany

We acknowledge support by the Open Access Publication Fund of Technische Universität Berlin.

ISSN 2192-7006   ISSN 2192-7014 (electronic)
SpringerBriefs in Quantitative Finance
ISBN 978-3-030-70883-2   ISBN 978-3-030-70884-9 (eBook)
https://doi.org/10.1007/978-3-030-70884-9

Mathematics Subject Classification: E40, E42, E43, E44, E50, E52, F55, 91-xx, 91-01

This Springer imprint is published by the registered company Springer Nature Switzerland AG
The registered company address is: Gewerbestrasse 11, 6330 Cham, Switzerland

Acknowledgements

We would like to thank Matheus Grasselli and two anonymous reviewers for thorough comments on an earlier draft of this text, which allowed us to remove mistakes and improve the presentation. All remaining errors are ours. We would also like to thank the Library Fund of the Technical University of Berlin for providing financial support for open access to this text, as well as Ute McCrory from Springer for efficient and pleasant discussions on this project. Ulrich Bindseil would like to thank the students of TU Berlin who, since 2010, have been asking the right questions and who have spotted many mistakes in the lecture notes that were used as input to this book. He would also like to thank many kind ECB colleagues for explaining to him since 1997 financial markets, payment systems, market infrastructures, and central bank operations. The views expressed are not necessarily those of the ECB.

About This Book

In view of the scale and scope of central bank operations over the last two decades, and the rich academic literature on monetary macro-economics, the title of this short book may appear pretentious. Aiming to deliver what the title suggests, while covering material that would usually fit into a one semester course, led to a focus on basic conceptual frameworks for understanding practical central banking, and in particular how we have seen it since the beginning of the millennium. While the burst of the dot.com bubble around 2000 led to a short preview on the zero lower bound problem, the years between 2002 and 2006 briefly restored what we call with some nostalgia "normal" times. Since 2007, central banking in developed economies has felt un-normal and uncomfortable, as most of the time it struggled with the zero lower bound (some central banks entering the underworld of negative interest rate policies), had to engage in large-scale asset purchase programs and lender of last resort (LOLR) operations, and as a consequence witnessed an unprecedented ballooning of central bank balance sheets. While forceful central bank measures certainly made a crucial difference for economies over the last 14 years, they have not yet necessarily been successful in terms of restoring full confidence that normality of inflation and interest rates will return in the coming years. This text is unavoidably inspired by the particularities of this period and aims at providing the basic tools for understanding what happened.

Amongst other content, **two types of content were sacrificed in the endeavour to keep the text short**. First, we rarely provide examples, real world numbers, or insights into public debates surrounding our conceptual framework for central banking. In view of the sheer endless diversity of actual central bank measures, experiences and debates over the last few decades, examples would probably have focused again and again on the few central banks of large developed monetary areas, although the experience of more than hundred other central banks has been as rich and interesting. Moreover, in the age of the internet and of a high degree of transparency in central banking, the facts and numerous debates are easily accessible to everyone, while what may be missing is a parsimonious conceptual framework. Therefore, instead of illustrating our book with selective examples and numbers (lengthening the text), we tried to present the material in a way that the reader can match herself with the easily accessible central banking reality in its full variety. In terms of overviews of actual measures and frameworks, and empirical analysis, a number of freely available publications can be recommended, also as they refer to further literature: Markets Committee (2019b) and Cap, Drehmann and Schrimpf (2020) both provide recent overviews of monetary policy implementation frameworks. CGFS (2019), and Markets Committee (2019a) review unconventional monetary policies and their effects on market functioning. The actual monetary policy operations of the ECB (conventional and unconventional) have been described in a series of occasional papers by the ECB, notably the ECB Occasional Papers Nr. 135, 188, 209, 245 (for example Sylvestre and Coutinho 2020). The Fed New York has published for many years an annual report on its market operations and balance sheet evolution (e.g. Fed 2020b). Financial stability issues are regularly reviewed in regular publications by various central banks and e.g. IMF (2020a). Central banks' lender-of-last-resort operations are less transparent, but there are a number of papers discussing policy issues relating to the LOLR function broadly, such as Domanski and Sushko (2014), or Dobler et al. (2016), while also providing some insights into actual cases. Bindseil (2014) is also a more comprehensive treatments of related issues, including examples and historical illustrations, and less condensed to the essential mechanics of central banking (although not covering international monetary frameworks).

Second, we do not aim at reviewing modern monetary macro-economics, although this could be considered as one major field of central banking, if not *the* field of central banking for the academic economic profession. Instead, we only refer to monetary macroeconomics briefly, and recall some of its basic conclusions, with a view to explaining how these matter for actual central bank operations. This seemed justifiable for three particular reasons (beyond that of keeping this text short): (i) the basic intuition of the links between macro-economic ideas and central bank operation is relatively straightforward, while the state-of-the art models used in today's macro-economic debates is not; (ii) there are good textbooks on modern macroeconomic theory, undergraduate introductions can be found in Burda and Wyplosz (2017), or Blanchard (2017), while more advanced texts are Woodford (2003), Lavoie (2014), Galí (2015), Heijdra (2017), or Walsh (2017); (iii) theory seemed to have been lagging practice since 2007, i.e. central bankers under stress needed to act with little help from academic literature to solve their urgent issues. Therefore, sometimes, new monetary macro-economic models encompassing non-conventional measures seemed to be ex post rationalizations for the academic world of what central banks were observed to be doing.

This **book addresses economists, students and central bankers** who would like to be introduced in a concise manner to actual central bank operations, i.e., real-world central banking as determining the central bank balance sheet, the flow of funds in the financial accounts of the economy, and central banks' related interest rate and lender of last resort policies. While the text has been kept simple and accessible, and the models remain basic, the readership who may benefit from the book goes beyond undergraduate students, as knowledge on central bank operations, financial accounts, and their relation to better known policy fields, is sometimes limited also amongst research-oriented central bankers and post-graduate economists interested in monetary policy. What is relevant in real-world central banking has also been inspired by the practical experience of one of us having worked in four different central bank departments over the last 27 years (the Bundesbank's Economics department, and subsequently the ECB's DG Market operations, Financial Risk Management, and DG Market Infrastructure and Payment Systems).

This text tries to be comprehensive in terms of reviewing **how central banks interact with the real world in general, and financial systems in particular**. Central bank balance sheets and the financial flows driving their evolution across time (and simultaneously the evolution of the accounts of the other financial sectors, as every financial asset is also a financial liability of someone else, and vice versa) cover an important part of this interaction. Therefore, throughout this book, we use the key conceptual tool of financial accounts capturing financial systems and allowing us to represent both passive and active central bank operations ("active" operations being those initiated by a central bank, such as open market operations, and "passive" being those initiated by other sectors, such as the recourse of banks to standing facilities offered by a central bank, the withdrawal of banknotes by households via banks, or the in- and outflow of foreign reserves in a fixed exchange rate system). However, financial accounts do not capture the entire reality of central bank operations. First, interest rates are crucial for monetary policy transmission, and this text will therefore also explain why and how operations and financial accounts, together with the interest rates set on central bank operations, determine market interest rates (Chap. 3). Second, the distance to default of private sector debtors, and what it implies for financial stability and central bank operations, depends not only on balance sheet figures, but also on a number of parameters outside balance sheets, such as asset price volatility, information asymmetries, and liquidity buffers of firms as determined by asset liquidity and the central bank collateral framework. Therefore, this text also includes a number of basic partial equilibrium models of financial stability and related liquidity flows and central bank operations (Chaps. 5 and 6). Central banking practice since 2007 has frequently been determined by such financial stability issues.

The book is structured through its chapters as follows:

- Chapter 1 provides the necessary basic concepts, such as the system of accounts of the economy, the main sectors, and the way these sectors are interrelated through financial claims and liabilities. A central bank is defined first by its balance sheet and central bank money is the central bank's basic liability. It is explained how both monetary policy implementation and lender of last resort issues relate to liquidity flows or "flows of funds" across balance sheets. Recalling the logic of financial flows at the most basic level is therefore the basis for the subsequent chapters.
- Chapter 2 develops further the role of a central bank and its interplay with commercial banks. Together, the two ensure the provision of liquidity to the economy, such that the real sectors are shielded, if possible, from portfolio re-allocations by households and institutional investors. We also disaggregate the banking system into two banks to represent deposit flows between banks and their impact on the central bank's balance sheet, and to distinguish between what we call "relative"

and "absolute" central bank intermediation. We then integrate deposit money creation by commercial banks into our system of financial accounts, and revisit some old debates, such as the limits of such "inside" money creation. We then explain the ideas of "sovereign money" and "full reserve banking" within our financial accounts, and discuss the recent proposals regarding central bank digital currency (CBDC).

- Chapter 3 provides an introduction to conventional monetary policy, i.e. monetary policy central banks pursue during periods of economic and financial stability and when short-term interest rates are not constrained by the zero lower bound. We sketch how central banks should set their operational target (short term interest rates) across time to achieve their ultimate target (e.g. price stability), and we acknowledge the multiple complications in doing so. We explain how balance sheet quantities relate to short term interest rates, and how the central bank can rely on this to steer its operational target. Finally, we explain the importance of the collateral framework and related risk control measures (e.g. haircuts) for the liquidity of banks and for central bank credit operations.

- Chapter 4 introduces the reader to unconventional monetary policy, i.e. monetary policy using instruments other than interest rate policies as described in the previous chapter, i.e. pursuing an effective monetary policy when conventional policies are not able to provide the necessary monetary accommodation because of the zero lower bound problem. We then discuss negative interest rate policies, and the debate around its possible unintended side-effects. We continue with a discussion of non-conventional credit and securities purchase programmes, and finally revisit the classification of central bank instruments in three categories: conventional, unconventional, and lender of last resort.

- In Chap. 5, central banks are put aside for a moment as we review simple models of financial instability, which will be the basis for the subsequent chapter explaining the role of central banks as lenders of last resort. We first recall that financial instability is mostly triggered by a negative shock on asset prices, which sets in motion a liquidity crisis with vicious circles. We develop the concepts of solvency "conditional" and "unconditional" on liquidity, apply these concepts to the stability of bank funding, and introduce the problem of bank runs. We subsequently show why asset liquidity in a dealer market deteriorates during a financial crisis; how asymmetric information can lead to a freeze of credit markets; how declining and more volatile asset prices drive increases of haircuts and margin requirements, and how these can force fire sales and defaults of borrowers. We finally discuss the interaction between these various crisis channels and the implied role of central bank liquidity.

- Chapter 6 reviews on this basis the function of a central bank as lender of last resort (LOLR). We recall some long-established principles of the LOLR and explain how the systemic role of a central bank creates risk endogeneity and validates Bagehot's intuition that for the Bank of England, "only the brave plan was the safe plan" in a crisis. We develop the main reasons why a central bank should act as LOLR: compensation of negative externalities, unique role of a central bank as an institution with unlimited liquidity, unique status as risk free counter-party making others accept to deliver collateral to it even at high haircuts, and its mandate to preserve price stability. Last but not least, we develop a bank-run model which highlights the role of asset liquidity and central bank eligible collateral. We calculate through a model variant with binary asset liquidity and uniform central bank collateral haircut, but then also introduce the case of continuous asset liquidity and haircuts.

- Chapter 7 turns to international monetary frameworks, and what global liquidity these different frameworks provide. We first recall arguments in favour of and against fixed exchange rate systems and then introduce two international monetary arrangement of the past which implied fixed exchange rates, namely the gold standard and the Bretton Woods system, and explain why both eventually failed. We then turn to international frameworks in the context of the current paper standard: fixed exchange rates, flexible exchange rates, and European monetary union. We explain the role of an international lender of last resort and how it provides more leeway in running fixed exchange rate systems. We show throughout the chapter how bank and central bank balance sheets are affected by international flows of funds and the balance of payments.

Although this is only an introductory, conceptual text, it is tempting to think about what to expect from its perspective for **central banking in the coming years**. Central banking in the coming decades will remain challenging. First, according to market predictions, central bank interest rates could remain close to zero (above or below) for several years, suggesting also that nonconventional measures will continue to be necessary, most of which will contribute to preserve or even extend the current scale and scope of a central bank balance sheet. The ability to provide monetary policy accommodation will remain crucial, and so will understanding monetary policy instruments and their mechanics, and how they affect an entire financial system.

Second, the future seems as vulnerable to financial crises as the past decades: after Covid-19, Governments will remain indebted, and solvency of parts of the financial and real sectors will be precarious, despite all the important monetary, economic, and regulatory measures taken. The combination of supportive central bank monetary and LOLR policies, expansionary fiscal spending, and temporary softening of obligations for companies to file for bankruptcy, were all strictly necessary, but will also come with future challenges, in particular if the recovery would be sluggish. Lender of last resort policies of central banks will remain important in the years to come, even in a favourable scenario. The framework provided by Chapters 5 and 6 on how liquidity and solvency interact, and why central banks matter for it, will thus remain relevant for years to come.

Last but not least, it is increasingly believed that central bank digital currencies (CBDC) will materialise (if this word is suitable for digital innovations) as a major innovation in central banking over the next decade (see e.g. BIS 2019), and that it may have pervasive implications for financial systems, that will have to be managed through adequate CBDC functionality. The financial accounts framework provided in this book is a good basis for understanding both the impact of CBDC on a financial system, and how to address related risks (Bindseil 2020). The previous major innovation in the form of central bank liabilities, the introduction of banknotes, brought with it great gains in financial efficiency, but also initially quite some financial chaos, as in the cases of Stockholm Banco in 1656, and John Law's Banque Royale in 1720. To end with an optimistic note, this can be avoided with the introduction of CBDC, thanks to our better understanding of central banking today, including how it interacts with financial systems.

Contents

Abbreviations

CBDC	Central-bank digital currency
ELB	Effective lower bound, see ZLB
IOU	I owe you
LGD	Loss given default
LOLR	Lender of last resort
NFC	Non-financial corporation
OMO	Open market operation
QE	Quantitative easing
SOE	State-owned enterprise
VaR	Value-at-risk
ZLB	Zero lower bound

Symbols in Balance Sheets and Tables

Sometimes capitalisation slightly changes the meaning of the symbol (e.g. upper case usually indicates stocks, and lower case indicates flows/shock of the same quantity), subscripts mostly denote ownership: e.g. E means equity, CO means corporate and E_{Co} corporate equity. The cases in which subscripts denote a time point are explicitly listed here.

A, A_t	(Real) assets value (at time t)
B	Banknotes ("Bad" in Chap. 5)
Ba	(Commercial) bank
C	Credit, claim
Co	Corporate
ca	Capital account transaction
cu	Current account transaction
CB	Central bank
D, d	Deposit (aggregate), single deposit or deposit shock
E	Equity
i	Nominal interest rate
$F(\cdot)$, $f(\cdot)$	Fire sale loss cumulative distribution and density functions
Fr	Foreign reserves
G	Gold ("Good" in Chap. 5)
Hh	Household
h	Haircut
L	Liquidity
n	Number of goods
m	Number of households
P	Price vector
$p(a,b)$	Price of a in terms of b
p_i	Price of good i in terms of the numeraire
$Pr(\cdot)$	Probability of ·
RR	Required reserves/reserve requirements
r	Real interest rate
S, s	Securities (state or corporate bonds), stocks and flows

St	State/government
U	Utility
W	Quantity of white-noise traded securities
X, x_i	Commodity vector, i-commodity within the vector
Y, y	Interbank lending, stock and flow
z	Bid-ask spread
ε_t	Standard normally distributed shock in time t
λ	Liquidity spread
π_t	Inflation in time t
σ	Standard deviation
τ	Term spread
σ_ε	Standard deviation of random variable ε
Φ	Cumulative distribution function of the normal distribution

List of Figures

List of Tables

Chapter 1
Economic Accounts and Financial Systems

This chapter introduces the system of accounts of the main sectors of the economy (households; non-financial corporations, the government; banks, and the central bank), describing how these sectors are interrelated through financial claims and liabilities. A financial system, consisting of commercial banks and the central bank, manages flows of funds originating from households, without these flows causing a need for the real sectors to liquidate illiquid real assets. The basic types of assets and liabilities are: real goods, gold, banknotes, deposits, bonds, loans, and equity. We explain how the shortcomings of both IOU and commodity-money based financial systems can be solved via establishing a central bank. A central bank is defined here by its balance sheet and central bank money is the central bank's basic liability. Both monetary policy implementation and lender of last resort issues relate to liquidity flows within balance sheets. Understanding the logic of basic financial flows is therefore the basis for understanding central banking.

1.1 Real Economic Sectors and Basic Types of Transactions

The first economic sector is the household. According to the United Nations (UN and EC 2009), a **household** is a group of persons who share the same living accommodation, who pool some, or all, of their income and wealth and who consume certain types of goods and services collectively, mainly housing and food. We can characterise this household in terms of its holdings in the n real **assets** of the economy. **Assets** are resources controlled by an entity as a result of past events and from which future economic benefits or service potential are expected to flow to the entity (EC 2011). Assets can be represented by a vector $X' = \{x_1, x_2, \ldots x_n\}$, in which gold coins are the n-th asset, i.e. x_n. For example, the household owns: $X = \{x_1$ chicken, x_2 cows, $\ldots x_n$ gold coins$\}$. To express the aggregate wealth of the household a unit of account is necessary.

© The Author(s) 2021
U. Bindseil and A. Fotia, *Introduction to Central Banking*,
SpringerBriefs in Quantitative Finance,
https://doi.org/10.1007/978-3-030-70884-9_1

Table 1.1 The household's balance sheet

Household accounts			
Real Assets	P'X	Household Equity	P'X

In principle every pair of goods has one relative price, namely a price in terms of the other good. For example, say p(Chicken, Cow) is the number of Chickens needed to buy one cow. Obviously p(cow, chicken) = 1/p(chicken, cow). Also p(chicken, cow) = p(gold coin, cow)/p(gold coin, chicken). Assume now that we chose the n-th good, a well-specified gold coin (like the Florentine ducat with a fine gold content of 3.44 grams), as unit of account. Let's simplify our notation, writing the relative price P(Gold coin, chicken) simply as p_1 and P(Gold coin, cow) as p_2, etc. In this case we have used gold as a numeraire.

A **numeraire** is a commodity whose price is used as unit of account. Dividing the price of the n goods by the price of the numeraire we obtain $n - 1$ independent prices, while the price of the numeraire in terms of itself is by definition one. We can represent all these prices by a vector of prices $P' = \{p_1, p_2, \ldots 1\}$ in which each good is expressed in terms of the n-th good, in this case gold. The total value of the households' assets is then P'X and we can represent the balance sheet of the household as in Table 1.1.

The left of the balance sheet contains the assets of the household, and the right its liabilities, which actually consist only in the household's own equity.

One heroic implicit assumption in the above approach (but common in economics) is that of universal and immediately executable prices. Reality differs from this ideal for two main reasons.

The first is **illiquidity.** Some assets are rarely traded, and to purchase a certain asset in a relatively short period of time (within a minute, within a day, etc.), one will normally have to pay (significantly) more than if there were a lot of time to purchase it. Similarly, or often even worse, to sell the good in a short period of time, one will have to accept a significant price reduction, relative to the price that could have been achieved with more time. Immediacy of execution has a price, measurable, for example, in the form of **bid-ask spreads**, offered by dealers, namely the difference between the price the dealer requires for buying a stock and the price at which the dealer sells the same stock. For this reason, one says that the dealer offers "immediacy services". As everyone can easily verify, in many used good markets (antiques, cars and other consumer durables), dealer bid-ask quotes are around 30–50%. In the most efficient parts of financial markets, e.g. US Government "on the run" bonds, bid-ask spreads are below 1 basis point (0.01%). Most other markets are somewhere in between.

The second main reason is **asset specificity.** A machine may have been tailor-made to exactly fit into the production process of a unique factory. Therefore, the value of the machine for the factory is much higher than for any other use, even with an unlimited time to sell. For instance, a very expensive and sophisticated machine used to test aerodynamics in the aerospace industry could also be used in the car industry, but with a more limited scope, as a much less sophisticated and expensive machine could fulfil the same function. A car manufacturer would buy such a machine only for the price of a machine fulfilling the functions it needs, as it does not need the most sophisticated functions used in the aerospace industry. Also human capital may be specific, as an employee may be an expert in a certain unique production process, or a manager in terms of knowing and being able to manage the psychological idiosyncrasies of the members of a specific team. The crucial role of asset specificity for economic organisation was worked out, in particular, by Williamson (1985).

Both distinct matters will play a key role in Chapters 5 and 6.

We now introduce two other sectors which we treat most of the time as one: **corporates and the government**. In the definition of the United Nations (UN and EC 2009), **corporations** are "legal or social entities [...] whose existence is recognized by law or society independently of the persons, or other entities, that may own or control it. Such units are responsible and accountable for the economic decisions or actions they take, although their autonomy may be constrained to some extent by other institutional units; for example, corporations are ultimately controlled by their shareholders". The simplified financial accounts of an economy with a corporate and government sector are shown in Table 1.2. The corporate sector will hold real assets, and as counterpart financial liabilities, representing the means through which the corporates have been funded. There is one major difference between the corporate and the government sector: in the case of the corporate sector, equity is also a financial liability, i.e. the equity is owned by e.g. households. In the case of the government, equity is a genuine own equity and not an external capital owned by another party (like household equity).

Table 1.2   A financial accounts system with the three real sectors

Household				
Real Assets	$E_{Hh} - G - E_{Co} - D_{Co} - D_{St}$	Household Equity		E_{Hh}
Gold	G			
Company Equity	E_{Co}			
Company Debt	D_{Co}			
State Debt	D_{St}			
Corporates				
Real assets	$E_{Co} + D_{Co}$	Corporate Equity		E_{Co}
		Debt		D_{Co}
State				
Real assets	$E_{St} + D_{St}$	State Equity		E_{St}
		Debt		D_{St}

Why is there a separate **corporate sector**, separated from households? Economic production and therefore welfare has been spectacularly expanded by the establishment **"capitalist" firms**, which have as liability both debt and equity (held by investors), and that as counterpart own a part of the real assets of the economy.

The reason for the existence of "capitalist" firms is discussed in Coase (1937) and Williamson (1985). Alternatives to pool ownership for larger scale industrial endeavours would be, for instance, the *labour-owned* firm (cooperative) or *state-owned* enterprises (SOEs). Both alternatives work to some extent, but up to now the **capitalist firm has overshadowed its alternatives in efficiency** for a large part of productive activity.

We can disregard growth, and assume that the amount of real assets in the economy does not change (except if asset value is destroyed through disorderly asset liquidation). A part of the real assets moves into the ownership of the corporate sector, and the household is compensated by receiving financial claims such that neither the net wealth nor the balance sheet length of the household changes. Of course, over time the creation of the corporate sector will make a difference: (i) it leads to a higher productivity and therefore to a steeper growth trend of the real assets held by the corporate sector (and hence the total amount of real assets of society); (ii) individual households will have different individual exposures to real assets, to equity and to debt, and therefore also their wealth will evolve over time differently, depending on how they positioned themselves.

The **corporate sector's need for real assets** is obvious as far as traditional industries are concerned. For example, nineteenth century growth industries like **mining, canal transportation, railways, clothing, breweries,** etc. all obviously had needs to heavily invest into real assets. In the financial accounts, we assume for the sake of simplicity that these real assets are transferred from households to the corporate sector. In reality, most of these assets are actually produced over time by the corporate sector itself. In the case of **sectors like IT or services**, the financing needs arise for the purpose of establishing intellectual assets or the necessary brand name capital. Significant work is needed before the assets obtain value (e.g. thousands of programming hours before a complex software runs smoothly and can be deployed to clients). In these cases, it is not physically existing real assets that are transferred from the household to the corporate. Instead, the firm uses its funds to rent "real" human capital and to transform it into intellectual assets.

The *raison-d'être* of the **government**, and how to design it, are the subjects of Public Economics. Generally speaking, the government should provide "public goods", i.e. goods with natural monopoly properties in which economies of scale in production are positive without limits, such as for security and defence, the legal system, the core of the monetary system, and some parts of the infrastructure. Moreover, the state may regulate market failures (externalities in production and consumption) and address acknowledged irrationality in human behaviour (e.g. enforce education and prohibit drugs). All this requires a stock of assets and employees. While the feudal state can really be considered as one enormous rich and powerful household, democracies could be considered being "owned" in a non-financial sense by the people. In the definition of the United Nations (UN and EC 2009, 62): "Government units are unique kinds of legal entities established by political processes that have legislative, judicial or executive authority over other institutional units within a given area. The principal functions of government are to assume responsibility for the provision of goods and services to the community or to individual households and to finance their provision out of taxation or other incomes; to redistribute income and wealth by means of transfers; and to engage in non-market production." The financial accounts of the government are less obvious than those of the corporate sector, as many of the assets of the government are intangibles, and its equity is not really measurable. Moreover, the government is often composed of various heterogenous entities (central government, regional government, local utilities run by municipalities, etc.).

1.2 The Financial Sector and Financial Transactions

We now introduce **banks** into the financial accounts. What do banks do? They undertake various activities, as summarised in the following list. Some banks were specialized to a subset of these activities, while others cover many of them ("universal banks"). The historical origins of banks and of the various banking functions are explained, for example, in Kindleberger (1984, 71–152).

The United Nations (UN and EC 2009, 76) uses for banks in our sense the term "Deposit-taking corporations except the central bank" and defines those as entities with "financial intermediation as their principal activity. To this end, they have liabilities in the form of deposits or financial instruments (such as short-term certificates of deposit) that are close substitutes for deposits. The liabilities of deposit-taking corporations are typically included in measures of money broadly defined."

Table 1.3 A financial account systems with a full reserve deposit bank

Household			
Real Assets	$E_{Hh} - G - C$	Household Equity	E_{Hh}
Gold	$G - B - D$		
Bank deposits	**D**		
Banknotes	**B**		
Claims to corporates	C		
Corporate/State			
Real assets	C	Liabilities to households	C
Banks			
Gold	**D + B**	**Deposits of Household**	**D**
		Banknotes issued	**B**

Table 1.4 A financial account system with a fractional reserve bank

Households		
Real Assets	$(E_{Hh} - G - C) -$ $(1 - \alpha)(D + B)$	Household Equity $\quad\quad\quad\quad\quad\quad E_{Hh}$
Gold	$G - \alpha(D + B)$	
Bank deposits	D	
Banknotes	B	
Claims to corporates	C	
Corporates/State		
Real assets	$C + (1 - \alpha)(D + B)$	Liabilities to households $\quad\quad C$
		Bank credit $\quad\quad\quad (1 - \alpha)(D + B)$
Bank		
Gold	$\alpha(D + B)$	Deposits of HH $\quad\quad\quad\quad\quad D$
Credit to corporates/state	$(1 - \alpha)(D+B)$	Banknotes issued $\quad\quad\quad\quad B$

Table 1.3 introduces a **deposit and a note issuing bank** into the financial accounts, which however only holds the gold in custody (i.e. this bank offers payment and security services). The two liabilities are identical in terms of financial accounts representation—they are only distinct in terms of technicalities of transfer and earmarking of bank liabilities to the claim holders (for deposits, a central ledger is maintained and the bank can see who holds what amount of bank deposits; for banknotes, there is no central ledger can be maintained). Such a bank would have to finance its running costs through fees it imposes on its clients.

In Table 1.4, banks can use the assets obtained through deposit and banknote issuance to finance investments. Assume here for the moment that (i) banks only lend to corporates and the state, and not back to households; (ii) banks still hold gold at a certain ratio α of their total assets, essentially as a self-chosen or imposed liquidity reserve; (iii) corporates and the state do not hold deposits. Assume moreover that the gained ability of the banks to provide credit creates new opportunity for the corporate balance sheet to expand, say because bank credit can finance projects that direct financing from the household can not because of the insufficient monitoring expertise of households. In Table 1.4 the corporate uses the fresh bank credit to partially acquire more real asset from the household.

1.2.1 Commodity Money, Financial Assets and IOU Economy

To understand the origins of central banking, it is worth recalling the merits of money in general and of financial money, in particular from the perspective of contemporaneous authors. Already Aristotle (1998, book I chapter IX) had noted that the inefficiencies of a barter economy can be overcome to some extent by the designation of one real asset as the medium of exchange—typically coined silver or gold.

In the early eighteenth century, this was described for instance by John Law (1705, chap. 1) as follows:

> Before the use of money was known, goods were exchanged by barter, or contract; and contracts were made payable in goods. This state of barter was inconvenient, and disadvantageous… In this state of barter there was little trade, and few arts-men…. Silver as a metal had a value in barter, as other goods; from the uses it was then applied to. … … What is meant by being used as money, is, that silver in bullion was the measure by which goods were valued: the value by which goods were exchanged: and in which contracts were made payable. He who had more goods than he had use for, would choose to barter them for silver… Silver being capable of a stamp, princes, for the greater convenience of the people, set up mints to bring it to a standard, and stamp it; whereby its weight and finesse was known, without the trouble of weighting or fining…. As money increased, the disadvantages and inconveniences of barter were removed; the poor and idle were employed, more of the land was laboured, the product increased, manufactures and trade improved, the landed-men lived better, and the people with less dependence on them.

As there is little evidence of societies really being based on barter, or in which money evolved from barter (Humphrey 1985; Graeber 2012, chap. 2), this should not be seen as a historical account, but rather as a reason why mankind developed other means to make trade possible. The use of a precious metal as money solved the problem of enforcement, but had various efficiency limitations, in particular for larger scale payments: structural and cyclical scarcity of the precious metal, heterogeneity due to imperfect coinage and usage, fragmentation of units used, weight, risk of theft and therefore cost of storage and transport. Therefore, credit instruments were soon developed to support trade. A **financial asset** is a claim of one economic subject towards another, for whom it is a **financial liability**. Financial contracts typically refer to unconditional or conditional cash flows to be paid in the future, whereby "cash flow" meant in the past settlement with species. The most basic financial asset is an **"IOU" for "I owe you"**—i.e. a promise to pay, which can be expressed in a numeraire good or any other specific good. IOUs can help to partially address the inefficiency of both a barter and of a species-based economy. In the words of **Thornton** (1802a, 75) the benefits of credit are many:

> "The day on which it suits the British merchant to purchase and send away a large quantity of goods may not be that on which he finds it convenient to pay for them." Without credit, "he must always have in his hands a very large stock of money; and for the expense of keeping this fund (an expense consisting chiefly in the loss of interest) he must be repaid in the price of the commodities in which he deals." Credit sets him "at liberty in his speculations: his judgement as to the propriety of buying or not buying, or of selling or not selling… may be more freely exercised".

The **problems of an IOU-financial system** with many agents and therefore multiple claims and liabilities lengthening agents' balance sheet are: (i) Complexity to keep a record of all the claims and liabilities; (ii) Credit risk and costs to monitor all claims; (iii) Possible contagion in case of late payments or credit events. This raises the question of netting claims, and/or eventually settling them in money. Two steps have to be distinguished: financial claims netting *without* any increases of exposures to specific names and financial claims *with* "novation", namely the possibility to transfer a claim on one debtor from one creditor to another creditor, which implies such increases of claims to specific debtors. The potentials of netting without and with novation have been described for example by Kindleberger (1984, 440) in the specific context of the European Payments Union (EPU) but apply universally to any multilateral netting and settlement issue. Multilateral netting is in any case a complex practical issue, and it is unlikely that many agents can spontaneously coordinate on it in a pre-modern environment. Netting through novation moreover requires that agents are willing to accept changes to the identity of their debtors—which will only be the case if the new debtors are systematically better than the old ones. If there is **enough species to settle transactions**, then of course such a situation would not arise. But merchants may have insufficient species reserves or transferring species as a means of payment may be very costly.

A way to avoid both the problems of species payments and of an IOU system, is to create **financial liquidity through a single high credit quality, multiple-unit IOU which is accepted by all as means of payment** and store of value, and which therefore plays the same role as species in achieving settlement finality of bilateral trades, without however any of its inconveniences. If this IOU has the highest possible credit quality, then novating financial claims towards it is always an improvement, i.e., can be regarded as "settlement" of the claim. Issuing these universal prime IOUs can be done in various ways, the only constraint being that the issuer must be considered to be of the highest achievable credit quality (such that novation is always accepted). The status of having the highest possible credit quality can be supported by a credible commitment of convertibility into species (i.e. into a real good), and this was considered necessary throughout most of the early history of central banking. The issuer of this universal prime IOU may be the state, a public bank, or possibly a state-sponsored private bank. In the words of Aglietta and Mojon (2014, 432–33):

> Because debts have to be settled in other forms of debts, there is a hierarchy of debts and, indeed, of the institutions that issue them. The central bank is the bank that issues the debt in which all other debts are settled. … the ultimate liquidity in a payment system can be a commodity minted by the sovereign (or a foreign currency), or it can be the liability of a financial institution empowered by society as a whole or by its highest political authority—the sovereign. This institution is a central bank.

To illustrate the mechanics of central financial money creation, Table 1.5 shows a simple economy with m households (or m "merchants"), each of which initially have equity A and real asset holdings A. Assume the households initially do not have a suitable medium of exchange, which limits their ability to trade with each other. The central bank is a 100% reserve bank, i.e. all its assets are in the form of precious metal coins.

Table 1.5   A full reserve central bank

Household i's accounts (i = 1…m)			
Real Assets	A	Household Equity	A +G
Gold	G − B		
Banknotes/Deposits	B		
Full reserve central bank			
Gold	mB	Banknotes/Deposits	mB

Table 1.6 A central bank diversifying its assets into government bonds and credit

Household/Merchant i's accounts (i = 1…m)			
Real Assets	A − S	Household Equity	A + G
Gold	G − B	Credit from central bank	C
Banknotes/Deposits	B +S +C		
Government			
Real assets	mS	Government debt	mS
Central bank expanding the monetary base			
Gold	mB	Banknotes/Deposits	m (B + S + C)
Government debt	mS		
Collateralised lending to privates	mC		

While this scheme may improve the convenience of payments, it does not solve the issue of netting and settling the multiple cross household IOUs if the amount of precious metals in the economy is structurally insufficient or subject to cyclical fluctuations. The availability of medium of exchange to ensure efficient payment and settlement is only increased if the central bank extends its balance sheet further by adding non-money assets, be they real or financial, i.e. by mixing into its assets elements of the previous schemes. The scheme shown in Table 1.6 assumes that the central bank in addition purchases some government securities (amounting to S per household) and by providing some collateralised credit to each household (C).

The asset mix and total amount of assets will have to respect the need of the central bank to remain solvent and liquid, implying that the share of liquid assets should be sufficiently large (i.e. nothing is as liquid in this context as gold species, as this is what the central bank commits to pay out to its creditors any time) and that the credit riskiness of the portfolio should be contained—through an adequate average quality of non-gold assets, and sufficient diversification.

Chapter 2
Central Banks

This chapter develops further the role of a central bank and its interplay with commercial banks. Together, the two ensure the provision of liquidity to the economy, such that the real sectors are shielded from flows of funds originating from household and investors. We also disaggregate the banking system into two banks to represent deposit flows between banks and their impact on the central bank's balance sheet, and to distinguish between what we call "relative" and "absolute" central bank intermediation. We then integrate deposit money creation by commercial banks into our system of financial accounts, and revisit some old debates, such as the limits of bank money creation and the role of related parameters that the central bank can set (not only the reserve requirement ratio, but also the collateral framework). Finally, we explain the concepts of "plain money" and "full reserve banking" within the financial accounts, and also discuss in this framework the recent proposals regarding central bank digital currency (CBDC).

2.1 Central Banks in a Paper Standard

Since their origins (Bindseil 2019), central banks have evolved considerably. Today, they have most of the time the following set of common characteristics: (i) monopoly over the issue of the legal means of payment; (ii) public control and in most cases state ownership; (iii) a clear public mandate; (iv) possibility to create the legal means of payment without any liquidity risk or risk of default; (v) deal only with banks and the government and not with corporates and households.

Table 2.1 summarises the financial relationships of a modern central bank with the other sectors. Practices changed over time: modern central banks withdrew from accepting deposits from corporates and households, and they normally do not provide directly credit to governments.

© The Author(s) 2021
U. Bindseil and A. Fotia, *Introduction to Central Banking*,
SpringerBriefs in Quantitative Finance,
https://doi.org/10.1007/978-3-030-70884-9_2

Table 2.1 Counterparties for financial operations for central banks

	CB Assets		CB liabilities	
Sector↓	**CB Credit provision**	**CB Securities holdings**	**CB deposits**	**Banknotes**
Households	No	No	No	Yes
NFC	No	Yes (rarely)	No	Yes
Government	No	Yes	Yes	Yes
Banks	Yes	Yes (rarely)	Yes	Yes

A paper standard is a monetary arrangement in which the central bank does not promise convertibility of its monetary liabilities into precious metal coins. Issuance of monetary liabilities is therefore less constrained, and the central bank cannot default on a convertibility promise, as there is none. In a pure paper standard, the central bank does not need to hold gold nor silver. If it also does not need to stabilise its exchange rate to any other currencies, then its assets may consist only in domestic financial claims, such as loans to banks and domestic securities.

Table 2.2 provides a stylized representation of the balance sheets of the different economic sectors. It does not distinguish between financial equity and debt. However, it distinguishes between financial equity and real equity (equity that is the financial asset of no-one).

Table 2.3 shows an alternative representation of the financial accounts shown in Table 2.2. It avoids the redundancy inherent in financial accounts shown in balance sheet format as it shows every financial position only once in a matrix, and not twice, i.e. not separately as a financial claim and as a financial liability. The first column shows the economic sectors from which to see each row a list of assets. The row with the list of financial sectors shows, in each column below the sectors, the liabilities. Besides the matrix of financial claims and liabilities, there is one column showing all the real assets of the sectors (second column) and one row showing the real equity positions of the sectors, i.e. the equity not being a liability to any other sector (second but last row). Some positions will be zero by definition: for example $F(5,1)$ should be zero, because the central bank should never have any direct claims towards households.

We should always remember that the following equalities hold:

- Σ real assets $= \Sigma$ real equity, i.e. total real assets of economy are equal to total real equity
- $\Sigma\Sigma$ financial assets $= \Sigma\Sigma$ financial liabilities (sum of all financial assets across all sectors equals sum of all financial liabilities across all sectors)
- Σ assets of one sector $= \Sigma$ liabilities of one sector.

Table 2.2 Financial accounts in a paper standard

Household			
Real Assets	$E_H - G - D - B - S_H - E_C$	Household Equity	E_H
Gold	G		
Bank deposits	D		
Banknotes	B		
Corporate/state bonds	S_H		
Corporate equity	E_c		
Corporate/State			
Real assets	$D + B - S_{Hh} + E_C$	Debt securities	$S_{Hh} + S_{CB}$
		Bank credit	$D + B - S_{CB}$
		Corporate equity	E_c
Bank			
Lending to corporates	$D + B - S_{CB}$	Deposits Hh	D
		Credit CB	$B - S_{CB}$
Central Bank			
Corporate/state bonds	S_{CB}	Banknotes issued	B
Credit to banks	$B - S_{CB}$		

2.2 Changes to the Demand of Financial Assets in a Paper Standard

In this section we will review what happens if households adjust their demand for financial assets in a paper standard. Two of the sectors shown in Tables 2.2 **and** 2.3 **are assumed to make choices**: first the **household** chooses to diversify its real assets into financial assets and determines the extent of this diversification, as well as the reliance on each of the three types of financial assets: bonds, deposits, banknotes; second the **central bank** decides on the split up of its monetary policy operations between outright (i.e. direct) securities holdings S_{CB} and credit provision to banks (as residual, $B - S_{CB}$). All other balance sheet positions are expressed in terms of these four choice variables, plus the initial household endowment E_H.

The household demand for specific financial assets is potentially unstable, as households may want to reduce their exposition to a debtor whose solvency they no longer trust by holding more liquid and safe assets. In the following representation gold is merged into real assets. Households could refuse to roll over debt securities and reduce their related positions (which we will identify in the subsequent financial account tables as flow s) and hold more deposit. Alternatively, households may

Table 2.3 Parsimonious financial accounts representation through financial exposure matrix

	Real assets	(financial liabilities of ↓) 1. Household	2. Corporate	3. Government	4. Banks	5. Central Bank	Total assets
1. Household	RA(1)	F(1,1)	F(1,2)	F(1,3)	F(1,4)	F(1,5)	RA(1) + Σ_iF(1, i)
2. Corporates	RA(2)	F(2,1)	F(2,2)	F(2,3)	F(2,4)	F(2,5)	RA(2) + Σ_iF(2, i)
3. Government	RA(3)	F(3,1)	F(3,2)	F(3,3)	F(3,4)	F(3,5)	RA(3) + Σ_iF(3, i)
4. Banks	RA(4)	F(4,1)	F(4,2)	F(4,3)	F(4,4)	F(4,5)	RA(4) + Σ_iF(4, i)
5. CB	RA(5)		F(5,2)	F(5,3)	F(5,4)		RA(5) + Σ_iF(5, i)
Real equity		RE(1)		RE(3)		RE(5)	
Total liabilities		Σ_iF(i, 1) + RE(1)	Σ_iF(i, 2)	Σ_iF(i,3)RE(3)	Σ_iF(i, 4)	Σ_iF(i,5) +RE(5)	

withdraw deposits from banks (which we will identify as flow d) and hold more banknotes if they fear banks may be insolvent.

The effects of these flows will depend on the reaction of the banks and the central bank. If the financial sector is ready to provide the necessary elasticity, then the financial flows related to changing financial asset demand of household can be absorbed without damage. If however the financial sectors do not provide the necessary elasticity, then the financial flows triggered by the households can cause economic damage.

2.2.1   If Financial Sectors not Ready to Compensate Missing Demand for Securities

Table 2.4 assumes that households want to reduce their corporate bond holdings by s, and that the rest of the financial sector is however not available to play any role to shield the corporate sector from this. For simplicity, we assume that the household wants to hold again more real assets. If neither the commercial banks nor the central bank want to react to a de-investment of the households from corporate bonds, then the corporates are threatened by **illiquidity**. Corporate (and government) assets are illiquid and specific to some extent, i.e. they have been made specific to the uses by the corporates (in the sense of Williamson 1985). For instance, a machine that has a certain value if used in a specific production will likely have lower value outside this production. In the worst case, the machine could have no value for other companies apart from the value of the raw materials it is made of. Therefore, when sold, it creates a revenue that is lower than the value the asset has in the balance sheet. In the short term to produce the liquidity needed to pay off the corporate debt that cannot be rolled over, they lose value and create financial losses, as captured below. The letter "f" stands for **fire-sale losses**. To capture the effects, we need to introduce a positive equity of the corporate sector, held by households. The financial accounts of the financial system (bank and central bank) in this example are not affected. They would be if the equity of corporates were insufficient to buffer fire-sale losses, and the fixed income liabilities of corporates towards banks would suffer losses.

Society now suffers from asset fire-sale losses of **f**. If s is the funding gap of the corporate created by the declining willingness of the household to hold securities, then the corporate needs to sell not only assets of a value s, but of a value s + f, to generate a liquidity of s. These losses reduce the corporate's equity, and eventually the household equity (as the household holds the corporate equity). This is a first example of how liquidity and solvency interact, and how illiquidity can cause damages to society.

Table 2.4 Real sector when fire sales are inevitable

Households/Investors			
Real Assets	$E - D - S_H - B - E_{Co} + s$	Household Equity	$E - f$
Bank Deposits	D		
Debt securities	$S_H - s$		
Corporate equity	$E_{Co} - f$		
Banknotes	B		
Corporate/Government			
Real assets	$D + B + S_H + E_{Co} - s - f$	Corporate equity	$E_C - f$
		Credits from banks	$D + B - S_{CB}$
		Debt securities	$S_{CB} + S_{Hh} - s$

2.2.2   Commercial Banks Absorb Security Flow

Now we assume that households want to substitute corporate bond holdings by deposits with banks and that banks are ready to use the related funding inflows to close the funding gaps of the corporate. Table 2.5 shows this case. The banking system acts as lender of last resort for the corporate sector by recycling the deposit inflow to provide more credit to the corporates as illustrated in Table 2.5.

The system of accounts in Table 2.5 assumes that the banking system is fully effective in extending its balance sheet to finance the corporate sector such as to avoid any economic damage. However, in reality, quick adaptation of the balance sheet of banks will come at extra cost: (i) e.g. the staff has to get extra pay for "night shift work"; (ii) additional resources may be needed in the form of expensive consultants and external lawyers; (iii) the additional risk taking associated with the rapid acceptance of extra exposure needs to be compensated, etc. The banks will charge these extra costs to the corporate at the expense of the profits (or, in stock terms, of the equity) of the corporate. Moreover, if the households were also to have doubt on the solvency of banks, they could convert their securities into banknotes. In such a case only the intervention of the central bank can avoid a financial crisis.

Table 2.5 Flow of funds if financial system absorbs flows and shields real sectors

Corporate/Government			
Real assets	$D + B + S_H$	Credits from banks	$D + B + S_{CB} + s$
		Debt securities	$S_{CB} + S_H - s$
Bank			
Lending to corporates	$D + B - S_{CB} + s$	Household deposits	$D + s$
		Credit from central bank	$B - S_{CB}$

2.2.3 The Central Bank Absorb Flows and Acts as Market Maker of Last Resort

Table 2.6 shows the case in which households want to shift exposures from corporate bonds into deposits with banks (flow s) but at the same time want to convert deposits with banks into banknotes (flow d) and the central bank provides elasticity and acts as market maker of last resort in the bond market.

The central bank issues banknotes demanded by households and purchases debt securities as needed. None of the financial shocks relating to the instability of the household demand for financial assets reaches the corporate/government sector in the sense that fire sales can be avoided.

Funding shocks reaching the real sector imply forced deleveraging (like in Sect. 2.2.1) or defaults, both of which are costly for society. A total shielding of the government and corporate sector from funding risks, however, would also be costly in the long run as it would undermine market discipline and incentives to improve productivity. An indefinite softening of the budget constraint is credited to be one of the main sources of inefficiencies in planned economies and of the reason for the ultimate prevalence of market economies in the twentieth century. At the same time an excessively hard budget constraint prevents long run investment (Dewatripont and Maskin 1995). The intervention of the central bank should aim at finding the optimal compromise between these two opposite risks, allowing for an appropriate amount of "creative destruction" for maximising social welfare in the medium and long run. From this point of view the central bank can be seen as a solvency regulator of the economic system (Brancaccio and Fontana 2013).

Table 2.6 Flow of funds if central bank absorbs all shocks

Households/Investors			
Real Assets	$E_H - D - S_H - B$	Household Equity	E_H
Deposits Bank	$D - d + s$		
Debt securities	$S_H - s$		
Banknotes	$B + d$		
Corporate/Government			
Real assets	$D + B + S_{Hh}$	Debt securities	$S_{CB} + S_{Hh}$
		Credits from banks	$D + B - S_{CB}$
Bank			
Lending to corporates	$D + B + S_{CB}$	Household deposits	$D - d + s$
		Credit from central bank	$B - S_{CB} + d - s$
Central Bank			
Debt securities	$S_{CB} + s$	Banknotes	$B + d$
Credit operations banks	$B - S_{CB} + d - s$		

2.3   Interbank Flows

So far, we have assumed that every economic sector (households, corporates, the government, the banks, the central bank) is in itself homogenous and can be aggregated without losing anything. This also implies that shocks (liquidity and solvency) would affect all individual households and firms equally within each sector. In reality, all sectors—except the central bank and the government, each of which are constituted by a single entity—are internally heterogeneous. In the case of **households**: some have taken loans and are thus leveraged, while others are not. Moreover, households have different asset compositions. Some own real estate (as the typical largest real asset position of households) while others have almost only financial assets. Finally, some households may have a lot of equity (are rich) while others may have almost none or even a negative equity (are poor). **Corporates and banks** have different liability structures, i.e. different shares of credit, bond issuance, and equity. Bank credit and bonds may have different maturity structures, etc.

Today's banking crises are typically not about shifts of deposits into banknotes, but about shifts of deposits between banks. We therefore need to adjust the previous financial account systems by introducing two separate banks—we obtain **Table** 2.7 as a result. This will also allow us in Table 2.7 to include an interbank market. We assume that the banks are identical ex-ante, and each represent one half of the banking system. The interbank market position between the two types of banks is set initially to Y, with bank 1 lending to bank 2. This could be the case because bank 1 has comparative advantages in deposit collection, while bank 2 has comparative advantages in originating and managing loans to corporates. We simplify the model above in the sense that we no longer consider securities issuance as a funding source for corporates, but introduce two new flows to the model. **Flow d>0** reflects a **deposit shift between banks** initiated by households. The flow may be triggered by one bank suddenly offering a higher remuneration rate, or by rumours about one bank having solvency problems. **Flow y>0** reflects a shrinkage of interbank lending, and may result from a change of business strategy by the lending bank, or that the lending bank believes that the borrowing bank is in trouble and that therefore credit riskiness of loans to it is perceived as too high. **Flows d and y both imply funding losses for bank 2, which consequently has to extend its central bank borrowing**. Note that if $d + y > B/2$, bank 1 will be in excess liquidity, i.e. without any recourse to central bank credit, bank 1 will have a claim on the central bank of $d + y - B/2$. In this case, the central bank balance sheet expands by the latter amount (Table 2.7).

These accounts allow us to define three important concepts.

- By allowing liquidity flows d and y to be compensated by heterogeneous changes of the recourse by individual banks to central bank credit, without lengthening the central bank balance sheet (as long as $B/2 - d - y \geq 0$), the **central bank provides <u>relative</u> intermediation to the banking system**.
- Once liquidity flows are such that some banks deposit excess funds with the central bank, thereby lengthening the central bank balance sheet (which happens in the above financial accounts when $B/2 - d - y < 0$), while other banks are

particularly dependent on the central bank, we speak of **absolute central bank intermediation of the banking system**. Normally absolute central bank intermediation can be avoided by setting a sufficient spread between the (higher) rate at which banks can borrow from the central bank and the (lower) rate of remuneration of excess deposits. Interbank lending allows the banks to collectively avoid the costs associated with this spread.

- By choosing to conduct its credit operations as "full allotment" operations, i.e. providing at a given rate whatever the banks ask for, the central bank can provide these intermediation services **passively**, i.e. it does not need to take any particular initiative for it. The limit to intermediation despite full allotment is central bank collateral availability. Widening the collateral set in a crisis specifically for the sake of allowing for more intermediation, or for providing confidence to markets that banks have large liquidity buffers, would be examples of **active** intermediation measures.

Finally, note that **interbank lending can be either positively or negatively correlated with household deposit shifts**, whereby the former case is detrimental, and the latter case supportive to financial stability. A **positive correlation** is likely if the main

Table 2.7 Household deposit and interbank lending shifts—with two separate banks

Households			
Real Assets	$E - D - B$	Household Equity	E
Deposits Bank 1	$D/2 + d$		
Deposits Bank 2	$D/2 - d$		
Banknotes	B		
Bank 1			
Lending	$D/2 + B/2 - Y$	Deposits Hh	$D/2 + d$
Deposits with CB	$\max(0, -B/2 + d + y)$	Credit CB	$\max(0, B/2 - d - y)$
Credit to Bank 2	$Y - y$		
Bank 2			
Lending	$D/2 + B/2 + Y$	Deposits Hh	$D/2 - d$
		Credit CB	$B/2 + d + y$
		Credit Bank 1	$Y - y$
Central Bank			
Credit to banks	$B/2 + k + y +$ $\max(0, B/2 - d - y)$	Banknotes	B
		Deposits banks	$\max(0, -B/2 + d + y)$

underlying factors are public news on a poor performance of the bank and possible related solvency problems. A **negative correlation** will occur if household deposit shifts are driven by factors which are independent of the actual credit quality of the bank and if the banks have no mutual credit risk concerns such that the interbank market can serve as an elastic buffer compensating exogenous liquidity flows. For example, a negative correlation generally prevailed in the euro area between 1999 and 2007, and a positive correlation was experienced particularly during the sovereign debt crisis, in which Greek, Spanish, Portuguese and Irish banks experienced both a cut-off of interbank lending and deposit outflows.

2.4 Role of Commercial Banks in Money Creation

2.4.1 Credit Money Created by Banks

To represent credit money creation in our system of financial accounts, we start from the simplest case of a financial account system with two banks and with all financing to the real economy being done through the banking system. Werner (2014, 1), one of the promoters of plain money (see Sect. 2.7 below), summarises the old question and the three schools in monetary economics about the ability of banks to create money as follows:

> According to the financial intermediation theory of banking, banks are merely intermediaries like other non-bank financial institutions, collecting deposits that are then lent out. According to the fractional reserve theory of banking, individual banks are mere financial intermediaries that cannot create money, but collectively they end up creating money through systemic interaction. A third theory maintains that each individual bank has the power to create money 'out of nothing' and does so when it extends credit. (the credit creation theory of banking)

Werner (2014) also presents an empirical test to conclude that the third school is right ("money supply is created as fairy dust produced by the banks individually, out of thin air", p. 1). **Table** 2.8 provides financial accounts to understand the issue. Denote by C_1 (C_2) the **credit money creation** by bank 1 (bank 2) to the households. We assume that households keep the money in the form of deposits with banks, but not necessarily with the same bank. Concretely, we assume that the household would split up its additional credit money holdings equally across the two banks, regardless of which bank provided the credit. Moreover, we assume that the central bank imposes a **reserve ratio of r** on the banks, i.e. banks need to hold a ratio of the non-bank deposits with them in the form of required reserves with the central bank. This duty implies an increased reliance of banks on central bank credit. For simplicity, we also assume that the banks have not issued any equity.

What could be the possible limits to credit money creation by banks on the basis of these accounts? Assume that credit claims of banks on firms and households are eligible central bank collateral, but that they are subject to a **haircut h**. The following

Table 2.8 Financial accounts with two banks and credit money creation (assuming $|C_2 - C_1| < B$)

Households/Investors			
Real Assets	$E_H - D - B$	Equity	E_H
Deposits Bank 1	$D/2 + (C_1 + C_2)/2$	Credit bank 1	C_1
Deposits Bank 2	$D/2 + (C_1 + C_2)/2$	Credit bank 2	C_2
Banknotes	B		
Corporate/Government			
Real assets	$D + B$	Credits from banks	$D + B$
Bank 1			
Lending to corporates	$D/2 + B/2$	Deposits Hh	$D/2 + (C_1 + C_2)/2$
Lending to households	C_1	Credit CB	$B/2 + (C_1 - C_2)/2 + r(D + C_1 + C_2)/2$
Required reserves	$r(D + C_1 + C_2)/2$		
Bank 2			
Lending to corporates	$D/2 + B/2$	Deposits Hh	$D/2 + (C_1 + C_2)/2$
Lending to households	C_2	Credit CB	$B/2 + (C_2 - C_1)/2 + r(D + C_1 + C_2)/2$
Required reserves	$r(D + C_1 + C_2)/2$		
Central Bank			
Credit operations	$B + r(D + C_1 + C_2)$	Banknotes	B
		Requ. reserves	$r(D + C_1 + C_2)$

collateral constraint applies **for bank 1 if it is the only bank that expands credit** (i.e. $C_2 = 0$). On the left-hand side of the inequality is the available central bank collateral after applying the haircut h, while on the right-hand side figures the recourse to central bank credit.

$$(1 - h)\left(\tfrac{D}{2} + \tfrac{B}{2} + C_1\right) \geq \tfrac{B}{2} + \tfrac{C_1}{2} + \tfrac{r(D + C_1)}{2}$$
$$\Leftrightarrow \dots \Leftrightarrow (1 - h - r) \cdot D - hB \geq C_1(r + 2h - 1))$$
$$\Leftrightarrow \tfrac{(1 - h - r)D - hB}{r + 2h - 1} \geq C_1$$

In the case of the euro area, $r = 0.01$ and h is approximately around 0.8. It is therefore plausible that $r + 2h - 1 > 0$. If $r + 2h - 1 < 0$, then the inequality would change direction when dividing by this term, and C_1 would be unconstrained. Therefore, to make reserve requirements and the collateral framework effective as a tool to prevent uncontrolled credit expansion by a single bank, the central bank must ensure that $r + 2h > 1$. Under this assumption, the maximum value of C_1 declines with increasing reserve ratio r and increasing haircut h. For example, if $D = 10$, $B = 1$, $h = 0.8$ and $r = 0.01$ (relative values broadly corresponding to the euro area), then the maximum value of C_1 is 1.8.

What happens if instead $C_1 = C_2 = C/2$, i.e., **if the banks engage in parallel credit money creation**? In this case, the constraint of the bank becomes:

$$(1 - h)\left(\frac{D}{2} + \frac{B}{2} + \frac{C}{2}\right) \geq \frac{B}{2} + \frac{r(D+C)}{2}$$
$$\Leftrightarrow \dots \Leftrightarrow (1 - h - r)D - hB \geq C(h + r - 1)$$
$$\Leftrightarrow \frac{(1-h-r)D-hB}{r+h-1} \geq C$$

If $r + h - 1$ is negative, as one should expect (and as it is certainly the case for the euro area), this equation is not constraining on C, as the direction of the inequality changes direction when dividing by this term. Only if the central bank imposes higher than usual reserve ratios in addition to high haircuts (say $h = 0.8$ and $r = 0.4$) does a constraint materialise. But, then, the bank would be collateral constrained even before providing any credit to households. In sum: even in combination, haircuts and reserve ratios are not a suitable tool for controlling credit expansion *if banks expand credit simultaneously and proportionally.*

However, limits to credit money creation arise anyway out of the **preferences of the household**. Bank credit money creation is costly in the sense that the banks will require a higher remuneration rate for the claims towards the households than what they offer in terms of remuneration rate of deposits (banks have to cover their operations costs and compensate their financial risk taking). Therefore, households will have a demand for credit money only to the extent that they see a particular utility attached to it justifying the costs. Extending credit to corporates would mean that corporates would use the extra funds for additional investments in real goods, which assumes that the productivity of these investments is sufficiently high. Extending credit to corporates for the sake of corporates purchasing financial assets is again limited by the requirement of this allowing the corporate to generate positive carry at sufficiently low risk. Therefore, again, this should not be sustainable and be relevant only in phases of speculative exuberance.

It is important to note that the credit money expansion by the bank has **no impact on the central bank balance sheet** in the financial accounts system above as long as the difference in the pace of additional credit provision by the two banks is not too large, i.e. **as long as $|C_2 - C_1| < B$**. Once this condition is violated, the length of the central bank balance sheet would expand because the bank with the more limited credit expansion would hold excess reserves.

The size of credit money expansion in any case affects the scale of possible deposit shifts, and hence the scale of possible recourse to the central bank to compensate for resulting funding gaps. Therefore, the length of the banks' balance sheets, and their ballooning through credit money creation, are relevant in financial crisis situations.

2.4.2 "Sovereign Money" and "Full Reserve Banking"

A number of monetary economists claim that deposit money creation by banks is one of the major causes of monetary and financial instability and recurring crises. Werner (2016) argues that by not understanding the problematic implications of deposit money creation, "the economics profession has failed over most of the past century to make any progress concerning knowledge of the monetary system". Some of these economists conclude that **all money creation should be undertaken by the central bank**. Banks would need to refinance through the central bank and through capital markets, but no longer through sight deposits (i.e. deposits that can be withdrawn any time without notice period). Two variants may be distinguished: First, Beneš and Kumhof (2012) return to Irving Fisher's Chicago Plan, which foresees essentially that banks have to hold the funds obtained through sight deposit issuance fully in the form of required reserves with the central bank (a sort of full reserve banking proposal). Second, Huber (1999, 5–6) explains the "plain" or "sovereign money" proposal, in which sight deposits with banks would be substituted by central bank money, i.e. banks would no longer have monetary liabilities. Huber (1999, 18) also explains the financial account implications of plain money:

> the credit claims of a bank on the loan-taking clients remain; the cash liabilities of a bank to the account-maintaining clients disappear, and the cash claims of the account-maintaining clients on the bank disappear equally; in exchange for the latter a credit claim of the central bank on the bank appears. These credit claims would be part of the assets on the balance sheet of the central bank, corresponding to the sums of non-cash money being registered on the liability side. (neither of which are the case today)

Also KPMG (2016) studied sovereign money (or as they call it the "sovereign money system") in a report commissioned by the Icelandic Prime Minister's Office. In this report, financial account representations are shown, and a survey is provided of political initiatives (e.g. in Switzerland, Iceland, UK, US) to study and possibly introduce plain money, and of academic literature.

In the financial accounts shown in **Table** 2.9, we interpret "plain money" as meaning that sight deposits need to be held at the central bank and we use a basic numerical example. The numbers are broadly representative of the euro area in 2018, if denominated in trillions of EUR (however with strong simplifications necessary to map the statistical financial accounts of the euro area as provided by the ECB into our simplified accounts, as well as rounding). The switch to a sovereign monetary system implies, in the stylised accounts of Table 2.9, a migration of 6 trillion of sight deposits from banks to the central bank.

The central bank becomes a much more important financier of the commercial banks, i.e. it becomes an intermediary between depositors and banks. The central bank balance sheet will lengthen, and central bank eligible collateral will become even more important for banks.

If instead we interpret sovereign money as full reserve money, as in the Chicago Plan, the financial accounts in **Table** 2.10 would be obtained.

Table 2.9 Plain money in financial accounts with illustrative numbers

Households			
Real Assets	6	Household Equity	14
Sight deposits	6	Retail mortgage loans	2
Banknotes	1		
Bank bonds	1		
Bank equity	1		
Corporate/state bonds	1		
Corporate/Government			
Real assets	8	Bonds issued	1
		Bank credit to corporates/state	7
Commercial Banks			
Credit to corporates/state	7	Sight deposits of HH	6–6
Retail mortgage loans	2	Bonds issued	1
		Central bank credit	1 + 6
		Bank equity	1
Central Bank			
Credit to banks	1 +6	Banknotes issued	1
		Sight deposits of households	6

Table 2.10 Full reserve money/Chicago plan financial accounts with illustrative numbers

Commercial Banks			
Credit to corporates/state	7	Savings and sight deposits of HH	6
Retail mortgage loans	2	Bonds issued	1
Required reserves	+6	Central bank credit	1 + 6
		Bank equity	1
Central Bank			
Credit to banks	1 + 6	Banknotes issued	1
		Required reserves of banks	6

The implications on the central bank balance sheet are similar to sovereign money: the **central bank balance sheet lengthens** and credit risk-taking of the central bank and collateral constraints are likely to become more relevant, unless the central bank expands **its outright holdings of low-risk securities,** as we will discuss further below for the case in which central bank digital currency would move the financial system in the direction of "sovereign" money.

2.4.3 *"Central Bank Digital Currency" (CBDC) Accessible to Non-Banks*

The idea of Central Bank Digital Currencies goes partially in the same direction as plain money but would be voluntary and is motivated from the perspective of efficiency of the means of payment, and not out of scepticism regarding the stability properties of bank money creation. CBDC would be brought into circulation in the same way as banknotes: on demand by households and corporate users, who could freely convert bank deposits into CBDC. Indeed, the internet and the use of mobile devices have transformed the possibilities how money can be stored and exchanged. Already today, a large share of money transfers is undertaken electronically, via internet banking, card payments or the use of e-money. Furthermore, new technologies for digital currencies have become available. Normally, electronic money transfers are based on commercial bank money, i.e., money is transferred from one commercial bank account to another. Only central bank account holders, i.e., commercial banks and a few other institutions (e.g. market infrastructures, governments), can hold and transfer central bank money electronically. Non-banks can currently do so only in the form of banknotes. CBDC would be, like banknotes, a direct claim on the central bank.

The literature in favour of CBDC argues: (i) It is more convenient and efficient to hold central bank money in digital form than in the form of cash. (ii) CBDC is more secure than commercial bank money, from a credit and settlement risk perspective. (iii) People's preference for money in digital form could lead to an undesired increase in the usage of virtual currencies (e.g. "stablecoins") in the absence of CBDC. Virtual currencies may create risks to price and financial stability. (iv) The provision of CBDC is cheaper for the central bank than the provision of cash. (v) Promoters of plain money argue that increased reliance on central bank money has various macroeconomic advantages, such as higher fiscal income for the state and a more stable financial system.

CBDC could be implemented in two forms: First, offering deposit accounts with the central bank to all households and corporates. From a technological perspective, this would not be very innovative, but just a matter of scaling the number of accounts offered. Second, the central bank could offer a digital token currency that would circulate in a decentralized way without central ledger, i.e., without the central bank knowing who currently holds the issued tokens. This would be more innovative, and would require more complex cryptographic techniques.

If households substitute banknotes with CBDC, then central bank and commercial bank balance sheets do not really change. However, if households **substitute commercial bank deposits with CBDC, then this would imply a funding loss for commercial banks**, i.e., lead to "disintermediation" of the banking sector. Sight deposits largely used for payment purposes could shift to some extent into riskless CBDC, leading to a loss of commercial banks' funding of equal size. Banks would have to try to offer better conditions on their deposits in order to protect their deposit base as much as possible—but this would imply higher funding costs for banks and a loss of commercial bank "seignorage". The central bank could aim at limiting the attractiveness of CBDC, through fees, or through a lower remuneration rate than the short-term market rate. In addition to the structural loss of funding for banks, there is also a financial stability issue. CBDC makes it significantly easier for non-banks to shift funds out of banks in the case of emerging general credit risk fears towards the banking system (although already today customers can easily shift their funds from one bank to the next). Contradicting this, some authors have perceived the occurrence of CBDC as **positive for financial stability**. For example, Dyson and Hodgson (2016) argue that CBDC

> can make the financial system safer: Allowing individuals, private sector companies, and non-bank financial institutions to settle directly in central bank money (rather than bank deposits) significantly reduces the concentration of liquidity and credit risk in payment systems. This in turn reduces the systemic importance of large banks. In addition, by providing a genuinely risk-free alternative to bank deposits, a shift from bank deposits to digital cash reduces the need for government guarantees on deposits, eliminating a source of moral hazard from the financial system.

Table 2.11 shows the creation of CBDC in a financial account system. The creation of CBDC has been split into two parts: CBDC1 which substitute banknotes and CBDC2 which substitute deposits with banks. The accounts also reflect that the central bank would, instead of increasing only its lending to banks, also increase

Table 2.11 Financial accounts with central bank digital currencies

Households			
		Household Equity	14
Real Assets	6	Mortgage loans	4
Sight deposits	$6 - CBDC2$		
Total CBDC	$CBDC1 + CBDC2$		
Banknotes	$2 - CBDC1$		
Bank bonds	$2 + S$		
Corporate/state bonds	$2 - S$		
Corporates/Government			
Real assets	8	Bonds issued/loans	8
Commercial Banks			
Corp/Govt bonds/loans	6	Deposits Hh	$6 - CBDC2$
Mortgage loans	4	Bonds issued	$2 + S$
		Central bank credit	$2 + CBDC2 - S$
Central Bank			
Credit to bank	$2 + CBDC2 - S$	Banknotes issued	$2 - CBDC1$
Corp/Govt bonds	S	CBDC total	$CBDC1 + CBDC2$

its outright security holdings. In theory, one could imagine that the central bank would, for example, absorb corporate and government bonds from existing stocks of investors, and that this will make it possible for banks to issue new bonds that investors will happily take to close the gaps created by central bank purchases. This case is captured by the bond purchase flow S below. Then, if S = CBDC2, the eventual difference for banks would consist in being funded more through capital markets than through deposits (due to the introduction of CBDC). Such purchases of bonds by the central bank would mitigate the risk that large-scale CBDC2 would make the central bank collateral framework a crucial allocation mechanism of the financial system and that central banks would need to accept almost the entire assets of banks as eligible and impose only moderate haircuts. In the case of large scale CBDC2, preventing the central bank from becoming involved in credit risk and credit allocation despite the lengthening of its balance sheet will thus depend on the availability of low-credit risk bonds, such as in particular central government bonds. If these are abundantly available such as to fully match CBDC2 in the central bank balance sheet, then arguably the central bank would not increase its credit risks, the banks would not become more dependent on central bank credit, the collateral framework would not become a more pervasive factor, and the consolidated state balance sheet (i.e., consolidating the government and the central bank) would not increase. All this, however, does not imply that banks would continue to play an unchanged role in the credit allocation process. The more expensive and maybe less stable refinancing through capital markets makes banks less competitive relative to a direct capital market access of corporates, i.e., will tend to reduce the role of banking in the financing of the economy. This is further discussed in Bindseil (2020), who also proposes to address the risk of large scale CBDC2 through a tiered remuneration of CBDC, such that large holdings of CBDCs are subject to unattractive remuneration.

Large CBDC2 could also undermine bank profitability: (i) **Central bank lending tends to be more expensive than deposits**, which normally can be funded at less than the short-term risk-free interest rate. Therefore, bank profitability could suffer, and banks would have to deleverage to some extent. (ii) If the central bank decides to address this issue through **purchases of securities**, this **does not help** either: capital market funding is even more expensive than central bank credit.

To compensate for the implied tightening of monetary conditions, **the central bank may have to lower its policy rate,** for a given inflation target and for a given growth rate. This would reduce the positive effects on central bank income. Another issue, also arising under the "plain money" proposal, is **collateral scarcity** of banks, because central bank credit has to be substantially increased. In this case, central banks that have so far had a narrow collateral framework may have to broaden their framework to also accept non-government securities and loans to NFCs as collateral to secure the enlarged structural credit provision. Recently, central banks have devoted growing efforts to analyse central bank digital currency, as documented by e.g. CPMI & MC (2018), Sveriges Riksbank (2020), the Bank of England (2020b), Bindseil (2020), ECB (2020e), Auer, Cornelli, and Frost (2020), BIS (2020). The implications of CBDC on the financial system and the economy have been assessed from a macroeconomic perspective in e.g. Grasselli and Lipton (2019), Niepelt (2020) and Keister and Sanches (2020).

Chapter 3
Conventional Monetary Policy

This chapter introduces conventional monetary policy, i.e. monetary policy during periods of economic and financial stability and when short-term interest rates are not constrained by the zero lower bound. We introduce the concept of an operational target of monetary policy and explain why central banks normally give this role to the short-term interbank rate. We briefly touch macroeconomics by outlining how central banks should set interest rates across time to achieve their ultimate target, e.g. price stability, and we acknowledge the complications in doing so. We then zoom further into monetary policy operations and central bank balance sheets by developing the concepts of autonomous factor, monetary policy instruments, and liquidity-absorbing and liquidity providing balance sheet items. Subsequently we explain how these quantities relate to short-term interest rates, and how the central bank can rely on this relation to steer its operational target, and thereby the starting point of monetary policy transmission. Finally, we explain the importance of the collateral framework and related risk control measures (e.g. haircuts) for the liquidity of banks and for the conduct of central bank credit operations.

3.1   Short-Term Interest Rates as the Operational Target of Monetary Policy

3.1.1   The Targets of Monetary Policy

The **operational target of** monetary policy is an economic variable, which the central bank wants, and indeed can control on a day-by-day basis using its monetary policy instruments. It is the variable for which (i) the policy decision making committee sets the target level in each of its meetings; which (ii) gives guidance to the staff of the

U. Bindseil and A. Fotia, *Introduction to Central Banking*,
SpringerBriefs in Quantitative Finance,
https://doi.org/10.1007/978-3-030-70884-9_3

central bank what really to do on a day-by-day basis, and (iii) serves to communicate the stance of monetary policy to the public.

There are essentially three main types of operational targets: (i) a **short-term interest rate**, which is today and was until 1914 the dominant approach; (ii) a **foreign exchange rate**, for central banks which peg their own currency strictly to a foreign one, usually a small or developing economy; and (iii) **a quantitative, reserve related concept**, which was in different variants the official operational target of the Federal Reserve of the United States in the period 1920–1983. However, how it was meant to be applied is not completely clear (for a deeper discussion of this topic, see Bindseil [2004]).

The **ultimate target** of monetary policy is the objective that the central bank wants to achieve in the medium or in the long run. It is the precise quantitative specification of the objectives established by the mandate of the bank. Currently there are two predominant ultimate targets:

- **Inflation rate**: usually defined as an annual increase of the consumer price index. It is the most common target for advanced economies and is used also in some emerging economies. In some cases, it is the ultimate target together with other objectives. For example, in the case of the Fed, the objectives spelled out in Section 2A of the Federal Reserve Act are "maximum employment, stable prices, and moderate long-term interest rates";
- **Foreign exchange rate**: in case of a currency peg, the ultimate target is the exchange rate, and all other variables, and the operational and ultimate target collapse into one.

Other ultimate targets, which have been applied in the past, or which are currently being discussed, include:

- **Monetary aggregates**: Friedman (1982) proposed to make a narrow monetary quantity the ultimate target of the central bank. A somewhat less radical variant was defined by the Deutsche Bundesbank with monetary growth as an intermediate target to pursue price stability (Deutsche Bundesbank 1995).
- **Nominal GDP targeting**. At least since Clark (1994), nominal GDP targets have been considered as an alternative monetary policy strategy to inflation targeting. Recently, Williams (2016) has advocated nominal GDP targets as they would have a number of advantages in a world with lower growth and lower natural interest rates.
- **Price-level targeting** has similarities to inflation targeting, but would compensate past deviations of actual inflation from the target with subsequent opposite deviations. Such an approach would reduce long-run uncertainty regarding the price level. For a survey, see Ambler (2009). Arguably the Fed adopted elements of price-level targeting in its recent decision of pursuing an *average* inflation rate of 2% by allowing an inflation rate moderately above 2% after periods in which inflation has been below 2% (Fed 2020d).

A central bank may have a **single or dual mandate**: for example, the ECB has the primary objective of price stability and other economic objectives are subordinate to that imperative (EU 2007), while the US Fed has, according to the Federal Reserve Act as amended in 1977, the statutory objectives for monetary policy of maximum employment, stable prices, and moderate long-term interest rates (although these seem to be three objectives, reference is made to a "dual" mandate).

The ultimate target must be precisely defined: for example, the ECB decided that "Price stability is defined as a year-on-year increase in the Harmonised Index of Consumer Prices (HICP) for the euro area of below 2%." and operationalised the target by aiming at an increase of the HICP of "close to but below 2%" with a medium-term orientation. Some, like Ball (2014), have suggested that it would be better to set the inflation target to 4%, at least in the possible new world of secular stagnation in which the zero-lower bound can easily constrain monetary policy (as further explained in the next section).

3.1.2   The Basic Natural Rate Logic of Monetary Policy

Thornton (1802b, 254) may have been the first to view central bank policy as a "bank rate" (Bank of England discount facility rate) policy, and analyses how bank rate policy should be conducted. Accordingly, short term nominal interest rates would need to follow the real rate of return of capital to control the expansion of money and hence achieve price stability.

Thornton also insists that the bank rate is always a sufficient tool to prevent over-issuance of money and hence inflation (except when usury laws constrain the central bank in this respect). Thornton's concept of a "rate of mercantile profit" is similar to the **"natural rate" of interest described in 1898 by Wicksell** (1898, 1936, 102) as follows:

> There is a certain rate of interest on loans which is neutral in respect to commodity prices, and tends neither to raise nor to lower them. This is necessarily the same as the rate of interest which would be determined by supply and demand if no use were made of money and all lending were effected in the form of real capital goods. It comes to much the same thing to describe it as the current value of the natural rate of interest on capital.

Figure 3.1 provides an arbitrage diagram (Richter, 1989) with two goods (wheat and money) at two points in time (today and tomorrow) to illustrate the natural rate idea.

By moving within the diagram from one good to another via different paths, arbitrage logic establishes some relationships between prices which are the starting point of the natural rate theory. Buying a unit of wheat for an amount p_1 today, and selling its real returns tomorrow, yields a revenue of $(1 + r)p_2$, while keeping the p_1 in money until tomorrow yields $(1 + i)p_1$. These two returns must be equal:

$$p_1(1 + i) = (1 + r)p_2$$

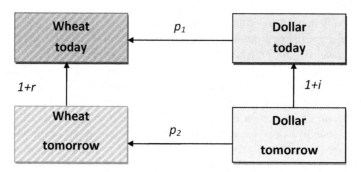

Fig. 3.1 Arbitrage diagram with real and nominal rates

Dividing both sides by p_1, and writing $p_2/p_1 = (1 + \pi)$, with π being the inflation rate, one obtains the Fisher equation:

$$(1 + i) = (1 + r) \cdot (1 + \pi)$$

The equation states that return on money must be equal to the return on real assets multiplied by the growth factor of asset prices. The latter equation is for small values of r and π approximately equivalent to $i = r + \pi$, i.e. in equilibrium the nominal interest rate should be the sum of the real rate and the inflation rate.

Above, **the real rate of interest is simply a relative price between "wheat tomorrow" and "wheat today"**. Its equilibrium value should depend on the preference of consumers and on the intertemporal production function. People normally prefer consumption today to consumption tomorrow, and the intertemporal production function normally produces positive returns, implying together that real interest rates are normally positive. However, in recent years, as well as in some other periods in history, negative real rates seem to have been observed (see the next sub-section).

Moreover, the simple arbitrage logic assumed that the inflation and the real rate of return were perfectly known, which is not the case. Starting from an initial state in which actual and expected inflation corresponds to the central bank's target and stable inflation expectations, $E(\pi_{t+1}) = \pi_t = \pi^*$, the central bank could preserve this state if it manages to keep the money (nominal) interest rate, i_t, always equal to the expected real rate of return on capital $E(r_t)$ plus the inflation target π^*. Wicksell's above quoted statement on the natural rate of interest assumes as starting point zero inflation expectations, so that the **natural interest rate** equals the expected real rate of return on capital goods, $E(r_t)$. If however inflation expectations are positive, then the relevant concept is the "**non-accelerating interest rate**", which is the rate that is neutral not to the price level, but to the rate of change of the price level, and this rate is equal to $E(r_t) + E(\pi_t)$:

$$i_t = E(r_t) + E(\pi_t)$$

The expected real rate of return on capital goods, $E(r_t)$, will vary over time, as its underlying factors varies. Therefore, the central bank also has to adjust the nominal interest rate across time to achieve stability of the inflation rate at its target level over time.

The nominal interest rate i_t is contractually fixed at the point in time t and is the nominal interest rate on money covering the period $[t, t + 1]$. The real rate r_t covering $[t, t + 1]$ is not yet fixed at t, nor is $\pi_t = (p_{t+1} - p_t)/(p_t)$ The general idea of the dynamics triggered by a perceived arbitrage opportunity is as follows (with i_t^* we mark the neutral rate):

- $i_t > i_t^* = E(r_t) + E(\pi_t)$ ➜ it is profitable to sell real goods and hold more money investments $\Rightarrow$ excess supply of real goods today ➜ disinflationary impulse ➜ actual inflation will fall below expected inflation: $\pi_t < E(\pi_t)$
- $i_t < i_t^* = E(r_t) + E(\pi_t)$ ➜ it is profitable to buy more real goods for real investment projects, hold less money investments (or be short in money, i.e. borrow money), ➜ excess demand for goods today ➜ inflationary impulse ➜actual inflation will turn out to be above expected inflation: $\pi_t > E(\pi_t)$.

It is not obvious how this dynamic process can be fully specified in a two-point-in-time arbitrage diagram.[1] Modern macroeconomic monetary theory aims at capturing such dynamics.

The **central bank can choose its inflation rate target**. For example, central banks often concluded that $\pi^* = 2\%$ is the optimal inflation rate (on models of the optimal rate of steady state inflation, see e.g. Schmidt-Grohe and Uribe [2010], who support low inflation targets, such as 2%).

3.1.2.1   Zero Lower Bound

An important limitation to the above-stated logic is **the zero lower bound to nominal interest rates implied by the existence of banknotes with zero remuneration**. If the interest rates on deposits were to be negative, economic agents could convert their deposit in banknotes, to avoid the loss caused by the negative interest rates. Due to the cost connected to the storage of banknotes, slightly negative interest rates can actually be applied by central banks. For this reason, some refer to an "effective lower bound", whereby central bank practice so far suggests that this effective lower bound could be of the order of -1%.

Assuming that the zero-lower bound would be strictly at 0%, the choice of the inflation target π^* must respect the constraint that $r_t + \pi^* > 0$. Since the real rate of return on capital r_t can be negative, for instance if the economy shrinks and the population is aging, a positive target inflation rate can be necessary to "lift" the non-accelerating rate of interest into positive territory.

---

[1]It is interesting to note that a similar issue arises in foreign exchange interest rate parity arbitrage. The main difference is that the exchange rate is a price that reacts immediately (as it is set in the most liquid financial market), while the price level in an economy reacts sluggishly to news.

The key problem associated with the zero lower bound to nominal interest rates is that it could make the central bank incapable of preventing a so-called **"deflationary trap"**. Indeed, if the non-accelerating interest rate i_t^* were negative ($i_t^* = E(r_t) + E(\pi_t) < 0$), but the central bank cannot set the nominal interest rate (i_t) sufficiently below zero, then monetary policy will be dis-inflationary. That means that—at least according to the simple arbitrage logic—inflation and inflation expectations will fall further, making zero interest rate policies even more dis-inflationary, etc. This is why some authors (e.g. Ball 2014) have concluded that in a world of low growth dynamics and low real rates of return, it is preferable to choose a higher inflation target (e.g. 4%) as a buffer against negative shocks that could push the economy into the deflationary trap.

3.1.3 Complicating the Basic Natural Rate Logic

The equilibrium relationship above reflects a number of simplifications. In the real world, at least the following five issues complicate the basic natural rate logic.

3.1.3.1 Different Concepts of the Real Rate

The price system will most of the time be **outside steady state equilibrium**. Prices and real rates of return on capital are constantly hit by exogenous shocks. This implies that one needs to differentiate between the expected (ex-ante) and the actual (ex-post) real rate of return on capital, $E(r_t)$ and r_t. For instance, the actual rate of return on wheat is affected by the unpredictable weather conditions over the next 12 months. Moreover, when non-anticipated price pressures (relative to expected prices) occur, adjustment of prices are typically sticky and react only gradually. Amongst other things, this implies that the **real rate of return on capital** will be distinct from the ex post **real rate of return on money investments**. Indeed, the fact that ex-ante $i_t = E(r_t) + E(\pi_t)$ does not imply that ex-post $i_t = r_t + \pi_t$. The real rate of return on money investments is equal to (ex-post) $i_t - \pi_t$. The real rate of return on capital is (ex-post) r_t. There is a third concept that needs to be distinguished, which is the **ex-ante real rate of return on money investments**, which is $i_t - E(\pi_t)$. This is the most frequently used concept when the term "real interest rates" is used in the media and academic papers. In an ex-ante arbitrage steady state equilibrium, this should be equal to $E(r_t)$. However, in reality, ex-ante adjustments to reach an arbitrage equilibrium may be imperfect and slow (e.g. the "time to build" argument), so that it is necessary to distinguish between the expected real rate of return on capital ($E(r_t)$) and the expected real rate of return on money investments ($i_t - E(\pi_t)$). **Table** 3.1 summarises the four concepts of real rates that eventually need to be distinguished, as they will, for the reasons mentioned above, not be identical. Note the assumption that the nominal interest rate on money is identical ex-post and ex-ante. This holds as long as debtors do not default.

Table 3.1 Four concepts of the real rate of interest

	Ex-ante	Ex-post
Real capital investment	$E(r_t)$	r_t
Money investment	$i_t - E(\pi_t)$	$i_t - \pi_t$

3.1.3.2 More Than One Real Good

In reality there is not only one real good ("wheat") which is at the same time a consumption and an investment good, but there is a **wide range of goods** with very different properties. Investment goods are supposed to determine the real rate of return on capital, while consumer goods determine inflation. Consumer and investment good prices are eventually linked, but such links are imperfect and lagged.

3.1.3.3 Funding Costs of the Economy Versus Short-Term Risk-Free Rates

Nominal funding costs of the real economy are not identical to the short-term nominal interest rate that the central bank sets. **Nominal funding costs of the real economy** can be estimated by producing a weighted average of funding rates, the weights reflecting the share of that type of funding in the total funding of the real economy. For example, for the euro area, **Table** 2.4 of the statistical annex of each ECB Economic Bulletin contains a detailed split up of lending rates for new and outstanding loans to various obligor classes (household consumer credit, household mortgage loans, loans no non-financial corporates, etc.) with volumes known from the Monetary Financial Institutions (MFI) statistics. Corporate and sovereign bond yields can be collected from information systems such as Reuters and Bloomberg. The weighted average nominal lending rate of the economy can be thought to reflect three main factors: (i) the quasi-risk-free short-term interbank interest rate which is normally controlled precisely by the central bank; (ii) The term spread in the risk-free benchmark yield curve; (iii) The various instrument-specific credit risk and liquidity premia. Credit risk premia result from investors requiring an additional return on credit risky assets, to be compensated against possible losses in case of debtor default. Liquidity premia result from investors requiring an additional return on assets which cannot be easily liquidated, compared to those assets which are highly liquid. Indeed, many investors may have to unexpectedly liquidate their assets under some scenarios, and in that case holding an illiquid asset will lead to losses, in particular if large amounts need to be sold quickly. In the presence of such premia, the challenge for the central bank is then no longer limited to the estimation of the expected real rate of return on capital goods only (such as to shift the nominal short-term interest rate across time in parallel to this), but in addition to adjust across time for the varying spread between the weighted average funding costs of the real economy and risk free short-term rates. Moreover, if the real rate of return on capital is low (as is likely the case in a crisis), and in addition credit and liquidity spreads are high, then it is likely that the central bank will reach the zero lower bound before being able to make monetary policy expansionary. To express this generalisation formally, define:

- τ as the **term spread** summarising the slope of the risk-free yield curve, i.e. the difference between the risk-free rate at the average duration of real economic projects (say five years) and the short end of the risk-free yield curve.
- λ as the spread between the weighted funding costs of the real economy and the risk-free yield with the same duration, i.e. capturing **credit and liquidity premia**.

What does τ and λ imply for the setting of short-term nominal interest rates by the central bank? Does the central bank have to set $i_t^* = E(r_t) + E(\pi_t) - \tau_t - \lambda_t$? If in a liquidity crisis, λ shoots up significantly, this would indeed have to be compensated by a corresponding lowering of the short-term interest rate i_t to ensure that monetary conditions remain unchanged. In economic and financial crises, the increase of liquidity and credit spreads may also add to the potential ZLB problem. However, central banks can also influence spreads through non-conventional measures, namely forthcoming LOLR policies (to moderate credit/liquidity spreads) and long-term bond purchases (to moderate the term spread).

3.1.3.4 Quantity Constraints in Credit Markets

It has to be kept in mind that the actual availability of credit to the real economy cannot necessarily be measured by contemplating interest rates alone (e.g. Stiglitz and Weiss 1981). Funding markets for some indebted companies can break down completely due to an increase of uncertainty and information asymmetries (see also Chapters 6 and 7). The role of quantitative funding constraints has been recognised as a relevant element of monetary conditions by central banks, and therefore central banks have started to systematically collect survey data to be able to monitor this element of the transmission mechanism. For example, the ECB collects on a quarterly basis qualitative and quantitative bank lending data (see the "Euro area bank lending survey", ECB 2020a) and data on the access of SMEs to funding ("Survey on the access to finance of small and medium-sized enterprises in the euro area" [ECB 2020d]).

3.1.3.5 Empirical Estimation Issues

The expectations theory of the term structure of interest rates (longer term rates as a geometric mean of expected short term rates) does not explain comprehensively movements of long-term yields. Term premia vary over time, and decomposing long-term rate changes into expectations on short-term rates and varying term premia is challenging (see e.g. Abrahams et al. 2016). The variability of term premia for nominal interest rates can be of a similar order of magnitude as variations in expected future nominal short-term interest rates. The same holds for the inflation component of nominal rates (i.e. its split up into expected inflation and inflation term premia, or inflation risk premia) and for its real rate component (split up into expected real rates and real rate term premia). Term premia may be regarded as a residual item also capturing, beyond the term risk premium, other effects not captured by the measurement of expected short term rates.

Laubach and Williams (2016) review different approaches for estimating real interest rates:

- The simplest way would be to calculate past average values of ex-post real rates (average nominal short term interest rates minus average inflation rates).
- More sophisticated statistical approaches use time-series filtering techniques that try to separate longer-term trends from short-term variations.
- Yields on inflation linked bonds can be used to extract future expected real rates. However, forward rates include a term premium that contaminates the measurement of the market perception of the natural short-term interest rate.
- The Laubach–Williams (2003) model uses a multivariate model that explicitly takes into account movements in inflation, output, and interest rates. The natural rate of interest is implicitly defined by the absence of inflationary or deflationary pressures.

Recent estimates of the natural rate using the Laubach–Williams (2003) model suggest that the natural rate fell from a 1980-level of around 3.5% in the US and 2.8% in the euro area to levels below 1% and to below 0%, in 2015, respectively.

3.1.3.6   Conclusion

The five issues above are the reason why the theory of optimal short-term central bank interest rate setting is complex, diverse and inconclusive, and also why central banks have large departments devoted to monetary policy analysis. Modern New Keynesian economics relies, as a starting point, on Wicksellian ideas, and tries to capture short term dynamics (e.g. Woodford 2003; Galí 2015). The New Keynesian approach has received important qualifications and has also been challenged from various perspectives (e.g. Cochrane 2011).

3.1.3.7   Two Extreme Examples from German History in Which Arbitrage Logic was Ignored

In retrospect, one can identify episodes in which the central bank was obviously way off a reasonable interest rate policy, and thereby triggered fatal dynamics of the purchasing power of money. German monetary history of the twentieth century provides two outstanding illustrations.

Inflationary central bank interest rate policies are best illustrated by the application of the 5% discount rate by the Reichsbank from 1914 to 1922. Applying the arbitrage logic above, this discount rate was far too low as of 1915. Indeed, as shown

Table 3.2 Reichsbank discount rate and inflation in Germany, 1914–1923

	Reichsbank discount rates (%)	Consumer price Inflation (%)
1915	5	35
1916	5	33
1917	5	25
1918	5	38
1919	5	58
1920	5	113
1921	5	28
1922	5–10	1025
1923	10	$>10^9$

Source Bundesbank 1976, 6

in **Table** 3.2 inflation reached 35% already in 1915 (essentially due to the extreme public demand shock associated with war mobilisation) and remained at similar or higher levels until it exploded in 1922 and 1923. The approach "(i) borrow money; (ii) buy and hold real assets; (iii) sell real assets in the future" was therefore a consistent profit-making opportunity without interruption for eight years. Actual inflation rates were certainly limited by the price controls for basic goods during the war years and would otherwise have exploded even earlier.

Deflationary central bank interest rate policies are exemplified by the maintenance of high nominal interest rates in the deflationary context of Germany in 1930–1932, as shown in **Table** 3.3. There were various reasons why the Reichsbank kept discount rates so high despite deflation: defending the gold standard and convertibility of the Reichsmark as prescribed according to International Treaties like the Dawes Plan and the Young plan, despite capital flight and a debt overhang due to reparation debt. However, having explanations for these interest rate policies does not change the conclusion that they were highly deflationary, illustrating the Wicksellian cumulative process in the opposite direction than during the period 1914–1923.

Table 3.3 Reichsbank discount rate and inflation in Germany, 1929–1932

	Reichsbank discount rates (%)	Consumer price Inflation (%)
1929	6.5–7.5	0.0
1930	4–5	−5.5
1931	7–15	−9.3
1932	4–6	−10.4

Source Bundesbank 1976, 6

3.1.4 Transmission Channels of Monetary Policy

We do not aim to cover monetary macroeconomics in any depth here, but only touch upon it very briefly to provide the link to monetary policy implementation. The monetary macroeconomics literature distinguishes a number of so-called transmission channels of monetary policy, i.e. how changes of the operational target impact the financial system and the economy so as to eventually reach the ultimate target of monetary policy—say price stability.

The most basic transmission channel that central bankers tend to have in mind today is **the interest rate channel** based on the Wicksellian arbitrage logic explained above: If $i_t > E(r_t) + E(\pi_t) \Rightarrow \pi_t \downarrow$; If $i_t < E(r_t) + E(\pi_t) \Rightarrow \pi_t \uparrow$. The following further transmission channels are often mentioned in the literature, whereby the first three channels are closely linked to Wicksell's arbitrage logic.

- **Exchange rate channel**: $i_t\downarrow \Rightarrow$ capital outflows $\Rightarrow$ value of the currency $\downarrow \Rightarrow$ Exports $\uparrow$, Imports $\downarrow$, $\Rightarrow$ Aggregate demand $\uparrow \Rightarrow \pi_t \uparrow$
- **Equity/housing price channel (Tobin's Q)**: $i_t\downarrow \Rightarrow$ Value of discounted cash flows from asset $\uparrow$, Asset prices $\uparrow$ and therefore above replacement costs $\Rightarrow$ Investment $\uparrow \Rightarrow$ Aggregate demand $\uparrow \Rightarrow \pi_t \uparrow$
- **Wealth channel:** $i_t\downarrow \Rightarrow$ Value of discounted cash flows from asset $\uparrow$, Asset prices $\uparrow \Rightarrow$ Wealth $\uparrow \Rightarrow$ Consumption $\uparrow \Rightarrow$ Aggregate demand $\uparrow \Rightarrow \pi_t \uparrow$
- **Balance sheet channel**: $i_t\downarrow \Rightarrow$ Asset prices $\uparrow \Rightarrow$ Equity of banks, firms and households $\uparrow \Rightarrow$ balance sheet constraints to expand activity $\downarrow \Rightarrow$ balance sheet expansion $\Rightarrow$ Asset prices $\uparrow$ and aggregate demand $\uparrow \Rightarrow \pi_t \uparrow$.

A more detailed overview of the transmission channels, with extensive literature, can be found e.g. in Boivin et al. (2010). The theory and empirical assessment of transmission channels is the key issue of monetary macroeconomics. Deciding on interest rate changes relies on predictions of transmission, so as to achieve to the best possible extent the ultimate target across time. Non-conventional monetary policies will partially rely on the same transmission channels, but partially also on additional ones.

3.2 Composition of the Central Bank Balance Sheet

The central bank balance sheets shown so far have been simplifications with regards to two important aspects that now need to be differentiated further.

Table 3.4 Several autonomous liquidity factors in the accounts of the bank and central bank

Bank			
Lending to corporates	$D + B - INV$	Deposits	$D - D_{St} + FR$
		Credit CB	$B + D_{St} - INV - FR$
Central Bank			
Investment portfolio	INV	Banknotes	B
Foreign reserves	FR	Deposits Govt	D_{St}
Credit to banks	$B + D_{St} - INV - FR$		

3.2.1 Autonomous Factors

Autonomous factors are those factors affecting the central bank balance sheet and the amount of deposits of banks with the central bank which are **not monetary policy operations**. They are not under direct control of the monetary policy implementation function, although they have a potential impact on liquidity conditions, and on short-term market interest rates. In the central bank balance sheets presented so far, banknotes were the only autonomous factor, but in fact there are other autonomous factors, which can all be integrated into the financial account model: (i) Governments often deposit their cash with the central bank, implying that on tax collection days, government deposits with the central bank may increase steeply, while they decline on days the government pays out wages of its employees. (ii) The central bank may intervene in foreign exchange markets, or act as foreign exchange agent of the government, and thereby increases or decreases its foreign reserves holdings. (iii) The central bank may buy or sell financial assets for investment purposes. (iv) the IMF may have credit lines with the central bank and may occasionally draw on those.

As illustrated in the financial accounts **in Table** 3.2, the starting level and fluctuations of any of these four autonomous factors affect the necessary recourse of banks to central bank credit, which can matter both from a monetary policy perspective and from a bank funding/financial stability perspective (Table 3.4).

3.2.2 Monetary Policy Instruments

Monetary policy instruments are the tools used by the central bank to reach its operational target. Central banks mainly use three such tools: standing facilities, open market operations, and reserve requirements.

Standing facilities are **central bank financial transactions at the initiative of banks**, on the basis of a commitment of the central bank to enter such operations at certain conditions. Three variants have to be distinguished: An **overnight lending**

Table 3.5 Overnight lending facility's and deposit facility's name in selected central banks

	Overnight lending facility	Deposit facility
Bank of England	operational standing lending facility	operational standing deposit facility
Bank of Japan	complementary lending facility	complementary deposit facility
European Central Bank	marginal lending facility	deposit facility
Federal Reserve	Primary credit facility Secondary credit facility[a]	Term deposit facility

[a]The Fed's primary and secondary credit have been introduced in 2003 in an attempt to overcome stigmatisation of the discount window (the overnight lending facility of the Fed). Primary credit is restricted to a limited number of well-capitalised credit institutions (Armantier et al. 2015)

facility allows banks to borrow at any time against eligible collateral at the rate specified by the central bank, with overnight maturity. It sets the upper limit of the interbank rate, as no bank would borrow at a higher rate than the rate offered by the central bank. A **deposit facility allows banks to deposit** funds at any time with the central bank on a specific account where it gets remunerated at a specific rate. It sets the lower limit for the interbank rate, as no bank would lend at a lower rate than the one it can obtain by safely depositing its reserves at the central bank. In the past central banks offered a **discount facility**: banks could **sell** certain short-term securities to the central bank at any time, whereby the discount rate specified by the central bank was applied to calculate the price on the basis of the securities' cash-flows. It was the main tool of central bank liquidity provision in the nineteenth century, but is no longer in use today.

Table 3.5 provides the relevant names of these facilities across some major central banks.[2]

Open market operations are central bank financial transactions with banks at the central bank's initiative, whereby two subtypes can be distinguished: (i) Outright purchases or sales of assets (normally debt securities) from banks; (ii) Lending (or "credit", "reverse" or "temporary") operations with banks. Loans are provided through well-defined procedures: in a "fixed-rate tender", the central bank announces the interest rate and maturity at which it will provide credit, banks then express the intended quantity they wish to obtain, and finally the bank announced a full or partial allotment. In a "variable-rate tender", banks are allowed to submit bids at different interest rates and the central bank decides on a cut-off interest rate.

Reserve requirements oblige banks to hold in a certain period (per day, or on average over a two weeks or one-month period, for example) a certain minimum level of sight deposits on their account with the central bank. Fulfilment is measured only on the basis of end of day snapshots (i.e. intra-day levels of reserves are not relevant). The size of the reserve requirement of a specific bank is normally set as a percentage of specific liability items of its balance sheet which need to be reported on a monthly basis. In the case of the European Central Bank, the requirement for each bank amounts to 1% of its liabilities to non-banks with a maturity below two

---

[2]BoE 2020a; BoJ 2020b,2020a; ECB 2020c; Fed 2020c,2020a.

years. Even if reserve requirements are zero, there is still a sort of reserve requirement in the sense that banks need to hold at day end at least a zero balance on their deposit account with the central bank.

3.2.3 Liquidity Providing and Liquidity Absorbing Items

Both monetary policy operation and autonomous factors can each be further subdivided into liquidity providing and liquidity absorbing. If an asset item increases (be it a monetary policy item or an autonomous factor), then, everything else unchanged, the deposits of banks with the central bank (i.e. their "liquidity") will increase, such as for example if the central bank purchases securities for monetary policy purposes, or if the central bank intervenes in foreign exchange markets to purchase a foreign currency. If a liability item increases, and all the other monetary policy items and autonomous factors are unchanged, then the deposits of banks with the central bank will decrease. This happens if for example the central bank collects fixed term deposits from banks, or if the circulation of banknotes goes up. Vice versa, if asset and liability items decline, the opposite effects on the level of bank deposits with the central bank will occur. In practical terms, the effect on deposits of banks with the central bank materialise because the banks are the counterparties of the central bank when the related financial operations are undertaken, and their accounts with the central bank are debited or credit as a consequence of the operations. Below, we will assume that the central bank offers an overnight lending facility and a deposit facility, but that it does not impose reserve requirements. When the control of short-term interest rates will be modelled, the differentiation between (i) outright open market operations; (ii) credit open market operations; and (iii) standing facilities will be necessary. The **Table** 3.6 reflects this slightly more differentiated representation of the central bank balance sheet, ordered according to the three main types of balance sheet items.

Table 3.6 The central bank balance sheet ordered according to the monetary policy implementation perspective

Central Bank	
Liquidity providing items	**Liquidity absorbing items**
Autonomous factors • Net Foreign assets • Investment portfolios	**Autonomous factors** • Banknotes • Government deposits
Monetary policy operations • Open market operations—outright purchases • Open market operations—credit to banks • Borrowing facility	**Monetary policy operations** • Fixed term deposits or repo • Issuance of debt certificates • Deposit facility
	Deposits of banks

What was labelled B (for "banknotes") in the previous financial accounts is now defined as "autonomous actors", being the following net sum:

$$Autonomous\ factors = Banknotes + Government\ deposits$$
$$-Foreign\ reserves - Investment\ portfolios$$

We netted autonomous factors as a central bank *liability* item. Defining "monetary policy operations" as the sum of all monetary policy operations netted as a central bank balance sheet *asset* item allows us to restate the balance sheet identity of the central bank as follows:

$$Deposits\ of\ banks = Monetary\ policy\ operations - Autonomous\ factors$$

If the central bank imposes reserve requirements on banks, then deposits of banks with the central bank have to be at least equal to reserve requirements. Central banks therefore have to set the volume of monetary policy operations as follows:

$$Monetary\ policy\ operations = Reserve\ requirements$$
$$+ Autonomous\ factors$$

The left-hand side of this equation is the "supply", and the right-hand side the "demand" for central bank deposits. The deposit supply by the central bank has to suffice both for reserve requirements and net liquidity absorption due to autonomous factors. Define as "liquidity absorbing" all central bank balance sheet *liability* items (except bank deposits), and as "liquidity providing" all central bank balance sheet *asset* items. Bank deposits can be interpreted as a "residual" central bank liability item: any increase of another central bank liability item leads to a decrease of commercial bank deposits, while any increase of a central bank asset item leads to an increase in central bank deposits.

3.3 Monetary Policy Implementation Techniques

We now illustrate three basic techniques of short-term interest rate control through monetary policy operations: the ceiling, floor, and symmetric corridor approaches.

3.3.1 The Ceiling Approach

In the ceiling approach, the interbank interest rate will be close to the liquidity providing standing facility offered by the central bank. The central bank needs to ensure (through the choice of the two variables it controls), with a sufficient margin, that

$$Open\,market\,operations \; < \; Autonomous\,factors \; + \; reserve\,requirements$$

In this inequality we use "open market operation" to designate the net stock of securities and liquidity providing credit operations of the bank ("net" of liquidity absorbing open market operations). "Autonomous factors" have been netted as a central bank balance sheet liability item. Given the implied scarcity of reserves in the system, **banks are forced to borrow from the central bank facility, implying that the rate in the interbank market will be anchored around the central bank borrowing rate**. In case of changes of the interest rate target, the central bank simply changes the interest rate of the liquidity providing standing facility. The approach relies on sufficiency of central bank eligible collateral, as otherwise the ceiling is not necessarily effective in constraining market rates. The set of financial accounts shown in Table 3.7 illustrates this technique.

This approach was standard during the nineteenth century, when banks had to take structural recourse to the central banks' overnight lending facility and the overnight lending facility rate determined market rates.

Table 3.7 The ceiling approach to monetary policy implementation

Households			
Real assets	$E - D - B$	Equity	E
Banknotes	$B + d$		
Deposits bank	$D - d$		
Corporates			
Real assets	$D + B$	Corporate Equity	E_{Co}
		Debt	D_{Co}
State			
Real assets	$E_{St} + D_{St}$	State Equity	E_{St}
		Debt	D_{St}
Bank			
Loans to corporate	$D + B$	Deposits of HH	$D - d$
Reserves of banks (incl. RR)	RR	CB borrowing facility	$RR + B + d$
Central Bank			
Borrowing facility	$RR + B + d$	Banknotes	$B + d$
		Reserves of banks (incl. RR)	RR

3.3.2 The Floor Approach

The **floor approach** has been used by all major central banks after 2009, and is now considered a new normal. In the floor approach, the interbank interest rate will be close to the liquidity absorbing standing facility (the deposit facility; or the rate of remuneration of excess reserves) offered by the central bank. The central bank needs to ensure (through the choice of the two variables it controls), with a sufficient margin, that

$$Open\,market\,operations\,>\,Autonomous\,factors\,+\,reserve\,requirements$$

Moreover, the central bank needs to set the rate of the deposit facility (or the remuneration of excess reserves) to the level of the intended policy target interest rate. **Given the abundance of reserves, commercial banks will be willing to lend them in the interbank market at any rate marginally higher than the remuneration of the deposit facility**. The financial accounts shown in Table 3.8 illustrate this approach. The central bank chooses the size of its outright portfolio OMO ("open market operations") such that $D + B > OMO > B + RR$.

Sometimes central banks have implemented **one-sided facility approaches with two facilities offered in the same direction** (i.e. either two liquidity absorbing facilities under the floor approach, or two liquidity-providing facilities under the ceiling approach). For example, during the gold standard, central banks often steered interest rates between two liquidity providing facilities, with *Lombard rate* > *i* > *discount rate* (the Lombard facility was the name of a collateralised overnight lending facility at that time; note that this was a ceiling system). Since 2005 the Fed has applied a floor system with *Interest rate on excess reserves (IOER)* > *i* > *Reverse repo rate*. These systems require that the more attractive of the two facilities is somehow

Table 3.8 The floor approach to monetary policy implementation

Corporate/State			
Real assets	$D + B$	Debt	$D + B$
Bank			
Loans and securities	$D + B - OMO$	Deposits of HH	$D - d$
Deposits CB	RR		
CB deposit facility	$-B - RR + OMO - d$		
Central Bank			
Securities	OMO	Banknotes	$B + d$
		Deposits banks	RR
		Deposit facility	$OMO - RR - B - d$

constrained in terms of access (discount facility possibly through scarcity of available eligible paper, IOER through limiting access to banks, excluding non-banks).

3.3.3   The Symmetric Corridor Approach

Under the symmetric corridor approach, which was standard in the years before 2008, the central bank offers both a liquidity providing and a liquidity absorbing facility, and keeps liquidity broadly "neutral" in the sense that ex-ante,

$$Open\,market\,operations\ =\ Autonomous\,factors\ +\ reserve\,requirements$$

This means that the probabilities that at day end (or at the end of the reserve maintenance period) the banking system will need one or the other facility are ex-ante symmetric, and therefore the interbank interest rate will trade in the middle of the corridor set by the interest rates of the liquidity providing and liquidity absorbing standing facilities. The central bank sets the rate of the two facilities symmetrically around the target interest rate. To capture the technique more precisely, assume the following daily timeline of events, as also summarised in the (Table 3.9).

- Every morning, the central bank determines its securities holdings S_{CB} such that $S_{CB} = B + RR$. B is the expected autonomous factors level, and RR the required reserves, and therefore, the expected level of bank reserves R is equal to RR.
- Second, interbank trading for overnight reserves with the central bank occurs, and the interbank rate is set as a weighted average of the two standing facility rates. The weights are the perceived probabilities of the banking system having to take recourse to one or the other standing facility at day end. As these probabilities are equal, the interbank rate should be in the middle of the standing facilities corridor.
- Third, the actual level for autonomous factors (B + d) materialises. The random variable d may be assumed to have a symmetric distribution and expected value of zero.
- Finally, at day end, the banks need to take recourse to one or the other facility.

Table 3.9 The symmetric corridor approach to monetary policy implementation

Bank			
Loans to corporate	D − RR	Deposits of HH	D − d
Reserves with CB (incl. RR)	RR	CB borrowing facility	max(0, d)
CB deposit facility	max(0, −d)		
Central Bank			
Securities (S_{CB})	RR + B	Autonomous factors	B + d
CB borrowing facility	max(0, d)	Reserves of banks (incl. RR)	RR
		CB deposit facility	max(0, −d)

The overnight interbank rate will be equal to the expected end of day marginal value of reserves, i.e. a weighted average of the two standing facility rates:

$$i = P(\text{short})i_B + P(\text{long})i_D$$
$$= P(OMO \leq RR + B + d)i_B + P(OMO > RR + B + d)i_D$$
$$= i_D + P(OMO \leq RR + B + d)(i_B - i_D)$$

Substituting $OMO = B + RR$ implies: $i = i_D + P(0 \leq d)(i_B - i_D)$. We can further simplify by taking assumptions on the random variable d: If for example d is symmetrically distributed around zero, then: $i = i_D + 0.5(i_B - i_D) = \frac{i_B + i_D}{2}$. The recourse to the borrowing facility will be max(d,0) and the recourse to the deposit facility max($-$d,0). If we moreover assume that $d \approx N(0, \sigma_d)$, then ($\Phi(\cdot)$ is the cumulative standard normal distribution):

$$i = i_D + \Phi\left(-\frac{OMO - RR - B}{\sigma_d}\right)(i_B - i_D)$$

This equation will also allow us to calculate the effect of deviations of OMO from $RR + B$ on the interbank overnight rate (assuming OMO, B and RR are observed by the banks before the interbank market session), which a central bank could rely on if it aims at an **asymmetric corridor approach, with** i* in [i_D, i_B], but i* $\neq$ ($i_D + i_B$)/2. However, any asymmetric approach requires the central bank to take into account, when choosing OMO, second-order moments of autonomous factors (i.e. not only the expected value of autonomous factors, but also the variance), which increases complexity. Neither the floor, nor the ceiling, nor the symmetric corridor approaches required this. Therefore, central banks only very rarely implement changes of their operational target level through a "liquidity effect" (i.e. change OMO volumes relative to autonomous factors) but through changes of interest rates of standing facilities. Academic authors have sometimes imagined that changes of the interest rate target would be implemented through liquidity effects, see for example Hamilton (1996).

In practice, a symmetric corridor approach also needs specification regarding the width of the corridor. Before 2008, corridor widths of 50 to 200 basis points were often observed. The choice of the corridor width is discussed e.g. by Bindseil and Jablecki (2011). Before 2008, the Fed's operational framework was the only one amongst major central banks that did not rely on a corridor approach.

3.4 The Central Bank Collateral Framework

3.4.1 Why Collateral?

Central banks conduct open market operations both in the form of purchases and sales of securities, and in the form of credit operations with banks. For the latter, central banks require collateral, i.e. the pledging of certain eligible securities, called collateral, to protect its credit exposures to banks. The central bank will sell the collateral in the market if the borrowing bank does not repay the credit.

The value of collateral required by the central bank will exceed the credit provided by the central bank because **central banks apply "haircuts"**. For each security pledged as collateral, the haircut will be deducted to determine the maximum amount of central bank credit that can be obtained against it from the central bank. The haircut will depend on the price volatility of the security, its liquidity, and possibly on its credit risk. The collateral protects the central bank from a default of the commercial bank. Once the bank reimburses the credit from the central bank, the collateral is returned in its full value. There are several reasons why a central bank should not offer uncollateralised credit. (i) the central bank must ensure transparency and equal treatment, and uses uniform policy rates, but the credit worthiness is not the same for all institutes. (ii) the central bank is not specialised in assessing credit risk. (iii) the central bank must deal with a high number of banks, and also banks with a low rating must have access to liquidity. Collateral solves all these problems to a very large extent.

The **collateral framework potentially influences the relative price of financial assets and thereby potentially the allocation of credit**, as Nyborg (2017) has recently emphasised. Bindseil et al. (2017) also review the economics and practice of a collateral framework. The long history of collateral issues in central banking is also discussed in Chapter 4 of Bindseil (2019).

3.4.1.1   What Makes an Asset Suitable as Collateral?

Financial assets should fulfil certain qualities to be suitable as central bank collateral, in particular: legal certainty of the validity of the pledge; minimum liquidity to ensure the ability of the central bank to easily sell the collateral in case of counterparty default; simplicity; ease of pricing (through market prices or reliable theoretical prices), etc.

3.4.1.2   Principles of a Collateral Framework

First of all, the collateral framework should ensure a high degree of protection of the central bank from credit risk. Second, it should ensure **sufficiency of collateral** to implement monetary policy through credit operations, i.e. collateral scarcity should not lead to a distortion of interest rates or constrain the access of the banking system as a whole to the necessary amount of central bank credit. Third, the collateral framework should ensure **sufficient access** of all parts of the banking system considered important for the transmission of monetary policy. Third, the collateral framework should avoid that the **collateral eligibility premium** is so high that collateral scarcity and the relative treatment of assets by the collateral framework could influence relative asset prices in a way that unduly affects resource allocation in the economy. A larger collateral set supports a lower collateral eligibility premium and hence reduces the risks of distortions. Fourth, the collateral framework should avoid pro-cyclicality: haircuts and eligibility criteria should be specified in good times in a conservative way so that they do not need to be tightened in crisis times.

3.4.1.3   The Risk Control Framework

The **risk control framework** for central bank collateral essentially consists in the haircut schedule and possible limits on the use of certain types of collateral. Gonzalez and Molitor (2009) and ECB (2015) present methodologies for deriving a central bank risk control framework for credit operations, such as haircuts, daily valuations, and margin calls. For example, the haircut scheme is a mapping of three features of each security into a haircut, namely (see ECB Press Release of 18 July 2013): **Rating**: BBB rated assets have higher haircuts than A-AAA rated assets (assets with ratings below BBB are normally not eligible at all); **Residual maturity**: the longer the residual maturity of bonds, the higher the price volatility and hence the higher the haircut; **Institutional liquidity category** of assets: The ECB has established six such categories, which are supposed to group assets into homogenous institutional groups in terms of liquidity. To keep the risk control framework simple, central banks rarely impose concentration limits on collateral portfolios, i.e. limiting the share of individual issuers, or the share of a certain asset type (concentration limits would have the advantage that in case of liquidation of a collateral portfolio, the price impact on the individual assets would likely be lower).

3.4.1.4   Methodology for Haircut Determination

The haircut setting of central banks tends to follow the principle of risk equivalence, i.e. after haircut, it should not matter from the central bank risk taking perspective which type of asset a bank brings as collateral. In case of counterparty default, the collateral submitted by that counterparty needs to be sold. This takes time and, for less liquid assets, a fire sale (i.e. a very quick sale) would have a negative impact on prices. The ECB classifies each security in one liquidity category, which is associated with a certain liquidation period, i.e. the period for which it can be assumed that the sale has no impact on prices. The haircut should depend on the price volatility of the relevant asset and on the prospective liquidation time, and possibly also on uncertainty regarding the initial value of the asset. High haircuts protect the central bank, but increase collateral needs for banks. This trade-off needs to be addressed by setting an adequate confidence level against losses. ECB (2004) set haircuts to cover 99% of price changes within the assumed orderly liquidation time of the respective asset class. Later, the ECB adjusted this method to cover with 99% the Expected Loss, which is the expected loss conditional on exceeding the 99% confidence level (i.e. haircuts were increased).

Assume an asset with a four week orderly liquidation period, and that the four week price change due to general volatility of the risk free yield curve is $N(0,\sigma_M)$; the uncertainty on the true asset value at the pre-default valuation is $N(0,\sigma_V)$; the liquidation price uncertainty stemming from spread changes (if it is a BBB asset, then the volatility of the BBB-AAA spread) and credit migration risks (the risk that the asset gets downgraded from BBB to e.g. BB with the associated price decline) is $N(0,\sigma_S)$. Assuming independent factors, the total uncertainty on liquidation value is $N\left(0, \sqrt{\sigma_M^2 + \sigma_V^2 + \sigma_S^2}\right)$. Call σ_T^2 the variance of the total liquidation value uncertainty of the asset. If the risk tolerance of the central bank has been defined as "preventing with 99% probability that the asset value at liquidation falls short of the last valuation minus the haircut", then haircuts need to be set at $\sigma_T \Phi^{-1}(0.01)$, where $\Phi(\cdot)$ is the cumulative standard normal distribution. If for example $\sigma_M^2 = 4\%$; $\sigma_V^2 = 2\%$; and $\sigma_S^2 = 2\%$, then the adequate haircut achieving a 99% confidence level is 58% since $\Phi^{-1}(0.01) = 2.33$ and $\sigma_T = \sqrt{4\% + 2\% + 2\%} = 2.83\%$.

3.4.1.5 Collateral Constraints

The quantity and quality of central bank eligible collateral limits the borrowing potential of banks from the central bank. Limits arise from (i) restricted eligibility (e.g. excluding particularly non-liquid and non-transparent bank asset classes and setting a minimum credit quality for the collateral obligor), (ii) conservative collateral valuation, (iii) haircuts, or (iv) quantitative collateral limits to address concentration and correlation risks (e.g. the share of a certain asset type in a collateral portfolio must not exceed a certain percentage). Assume the bank balance sheet in **Table** 3.10, with two liabilities, household deposits and central bank credit, and two assets, loans and securities. Assume also that the central bank imposes a haircut of h_1 on loans to corporates and of h_2 on securities, with $1 > h_1 > h_2 > 0$. Collateral value after haircuts (or central bank credit potential) is for loans $(1 - h_1)L$ and for securities $(1 - h_2)S$.

The maximum borrowing of this bank from the central bank is the value of loans after haircut and the value of securities after haircut, i.e.: $(1 - h_1)L + (1 - h_2)S$. The actual borrowing from the central bank, CB, must not exceed this, i.e.:

$$L + S - D + d \leq (1 - h_1)L + (1 - h_2)S$$

This implies that the bank will hit the collateral constraint when deposit outflows exceed $d^* = (1 - h_1)L + (1 - h_2)S - (L + S - D) = D - h_1L - h_2S$, and could

Table 3.10 Bank balance sheet to illustrate collateral constraints

Bank			
Loans to corporates	L	Household deposits	D − d
Securities holdings	S	Credit from central bank	L + S − D + d

default unless it finds alternative funding or is able to fire-sell assets. For example, in the case of the euro area, out of approximately EUR 30 trillion of aggregated bank assets, the value of central bank eligible collateral after haircuts that could be

Chapter 4
Unconventional Monetary Policy

This chapter introduces the reader to unconventional monetary policy, i.e. monetary policy using instruments going beyond the steering of short-term interest rates as described in the previous chapter. We start by providing the rationale of unconventional monetary policy, i.e. essentially pursuing an effective monetary policy when conventional policies are not able to provide the necessary monetary accommodation because of the zero lower bound. We then discuss negative interest rate policies, and explain why rates slightly below zero have proven to be feasible despite the existence of banknotes. We also discuss possible unintended side-effects of negative interest rates. We continue with a discussion of non-conventional credit operations: lengthening of their duration, the use of fixed-rate full allotment, the widening of the access of counterparties to the central bank's credit operation, targeted operations, credit in foreign currency, and widening the collateral set. Finally, we turn to the purposes and effects of securities purchase programmes. We end the chapter by revisiting the classification of central bank instruments in three categories: conventional, unconventional, and lender of last resort.

4.1 Rationale and Definition of "Unconventional" Monetary Policy

Chapter 3 introduced the basic Wicksellian logic, according to which there is a "neutral" or "non-accelerating" short-term risk-free interest rate i*, such that if $i_t > i_t^* \Rightarrow \pi_t \downarrow$; If $i_t < i_t^* \Rightarrow \pi_t \uparrow$ or, in words, if the actual short-term risk-free rate is below the neutral level, inflation will increase, while in the opposite case inflation will decrease. In the most basic version, the neutral rate is simply the sum of the expected real rate and the expected inflation rate, i.e. $i_t^* = E(r_t) + E(\pi_t)$. If however the key issue is the funding costs of the real economy, and not just an abstract risk free interest rate, then it is more correct to define the neutral interest rate as: $i_t^* = E(r_t) +$

© The Author(s) 2021
U. Bindseil and A. Fotia, *Introduction to Central Banking*,
SpringerBriefs in Quantitative Finance,
https://doi.org/10.1007/978-3-030-70884-9_4

$E(\pi_t) - \tau - \lambda$, with τ being a measure of the term spread and λ being a measure of the liquidity and credit risk spreads between the average short-term funding costs of the real economy and the short-term risk-free interest rate. The latter will increase in a financial crisis beyond normal levels and needs to be addressed through an additional easing of monetary policy.

In a **financial crisis,** with the associated economic slowdown, and starting from the low structural growth as prevailing in Japan or Europe, expected growth will easily be zero or negative, also implying low or negative real interest rates. If in addition, credit and liquidity spreads increase by 100 or 200 basis points relative to normal levels, as happened in 2008, and expected inflation is also close to zero, then the neutral interest rate i_t^* will be negative, meaning that an inflationary impulse will require either negative nominal interest rates, or the combination of zero/negative interest rates with "non-conventional" measures that will exert downward pressure on τ and λ. Downward pressure on τ can be achieved through forward guidance[1] (committing to hold rates low for long) and through outright purchase programs of long term fixed rate securities to compress term spreads. Downward pressure on λ can be achieved through so-called credit-easing measures, including purchases of less liquid and more credit risky securities, and strengthening the lender of last resort (LOLR) support to the banking system such as to reduce perceived funding liquidity risks of banks. In this chapter, such non-conventional monetary policies will be discussed, whereby policies relating to the LOLR will be dealt with in Chapter 7.

Non-conventional monetary policy measures are typically considered to have some potentially negative side effects, while short-term interest rate policies in positive territory do not. For this reason, non-conventional measures are used only if unavoidable, i.e. when $i_t^* < 0$, i.e. when short-term interest rate policies alone are no longer sufficient. Negative side effects are likely to increase with the intensity of measures, such that combining different measures may often be optimal to achieve the adequate overall stance of monetary policy. We can think of each non-conventional measure as having (i) a fixed set up /transition cost (need to analyse, specify, decide, communicate new measure); and (ii) an increasing marginal cost from "distortions" it creates.

It appears that **central banks have assessed the relative costs of the different unconditional measures differently**: for example, the Fed and the Bank of England have not hesitated to conduct large scale asset purchase programs as of 2009 but have not tried negative interest rates. In contrast, the ECB has taken a while before launching a true "quantitative easing" asset purchase program, but did not hesitate to move interest rates into negative territory. Of course, the perceived negative side effects of non-conventional measures always depend on circumstances, i.e. may be different from one jurisdiction to another, or from one episode to another.

The reasoning above assumes that the choice and specification of non-standard measures can basically be mapped into a single number: the additional accommodation needed beyond the zero lower bound. However, one may question this, and

---

[1] A more detailed treatment of forward guidance can be found in e.g. Filardo and Hofmann (2014), Campbell Evans et al. (2012), and Swanson (2017).

instead see non-trivial issues in the interaction of non-standard measures that imply that one cannot just add up the accommodation that each measure brings.

4.2   Negative Interest Rate Policy (NIRP)

Four European central banks have applied NIRP in recent years, namely those of Denmark, Switzerland, Sweden and the euro area (for a survey of the implementation of NIRP by these central banks, see e.g. Bech and Malkhozov (2016). In addition, the Bank of Japan introduced NIRP in early 2016. In principle, the rationale for applying negative rates under some circumstances is obvious from the Wicksellian logic above. It could be argued that in 2008, the policy-adequate short-term interest rate would have been as low as between -3 to -5%, i.e. if central banks had been able to implement negative rates at these levels, the crisis would have been more short-lived (avoiding the large scale economic contraction and associated welfare damage) and further non-conventional monetary policies (such as large scale asset purchase programs) with their complexities and side effects would not have been needed. Strong supporters of negative interest rates as an obvious policy tool are for instance Buiter (2009) and Rogoff (2017), who also discuss how to make negative rates possible.

4.2.1   Reasons for a Lower Bound

4.2.1.1   Lower Bound Created by the Zero Remuneration of Banknotes

Deeply negative interest rates should eventually lead to an explosion of the demand for banknotes, as banknotes have a zero remuneration. Indeed, it could be argued that all economic agents (banks, investors, households) can escape negative interest rates by substituting negatively remunerated financial assets with banknotes (which have zero remuneration). This is a powerful and obvious argument against deeply negative interest rates, and the only solution to it would be to discontinue the existence of physical banknotes, e.g. by fully replacing them with central bank digital currency, which could be remunerated negatively when needed. However, critics argue that this would create a tool for central banks to expropriate savers (by imposing negative interest rates, see e.g. Bindseil et al. (2015) and that discontinuing banknotes would also destroy, a la George Orwell's "1984", the freedom provided by anonymous payments. In addition, banknotes are resilient to cyber-attacks and power outages and they score high in terms of financial inclusion, as they do not require even a mobile phone. These arguments prevail for the time being in most countries, and therefore banknotes will continue to limit the scope for negative interest rates to the levels reached over the last few years, i.e. not lower than around -100 basis points. This seems to be the level at which banknote demand could start to have substantial momentum and undermine the effectiveness of negative interest rates. As in the case of a central bank digital currency undermining household deposits with banks seen in section 2.8, a ballooning of central bank money holdings of households would imply that banks would lose large amounts of deposits and become more and more dependent on central bank credit. This would deplete collateral buffers and could put banks under liquidity stress, making it unlikely that bank lending rates will decline, i.e. undermining the effectiveness of NIRP. Banks may not want to pass on negative rates to household deposits to avoid triggering such a run on deposits. However, then, banks' profitability suffers, as discussed further under point 2 below. In principle, the banknote hoarding argument also applies, for example, to banks, who could, in an environment of excess reserves, such as prevailing typically in the negative interest rate countries, start to hoard cash.

In the financial accounts in Table 4.1, we assume that both households and banks started to hoard cash as a consequence of negative interest rate policies. Efficient arbitrage would allow asset holders to fully escape from negative asset remuneration, fully undermining the transmission of negative central bank rates to asset yields. These financial accounts also show the case when the cash hoarding goes so far as to switch back (despite the QE program captured by S) the banks' excess reserves into a liquidity deficit, implying growing needs of central bank credit, eventually creating potential liquidity stress on banks.

Table 4.1 Banknotes hording under negative interest rate policies of the central bank

Households			
Real Assets	$E_H - D - B$	Equity	E_H
Bank deposits	$D - d$		
Banknotes	$B + d$		
Corporates/State			
Real assets	$D + B$	Debt	$D + B$
Commercial Banks			
Credit to corp/govt	$D + B - S_{CB}$	Deposits of Hh	$D - d$
Reserves with CB	$\max(0, S_{CB} - B - y - d)$	Credit from CB	$\max(0, -(S_{CB} - B - y - d))$
Banknotes	y		
Central Bank			
Securities	S_{CB}	Banknotes	$B + y + d$
Credit from CB	$\max(0, -(S_{CB} - B - y - d))$	Deposits banks	$\max(0, S_{CB} - B - y - d)$

4.2.1.2 Lower Bound Due to Negative Effects on Profitability of Banks

It has been argued that negative rates undermine bank profitability and undermine the transmission of negative rates as banks would be unable to pass on negative rates to retail depositors—see e.g. Bech, and Malkhozov (2016, 39–40), or Brunnermeier and Koby (2019)

Most central banks applying NIRP have acknowledged the particular effects of negatively remunerated excess reserves combined with an unwillingness/inability of banks to pass on negative rates to retail deposits through an innovation in their operational framework: so-called **excess reserves tiering systems which exempt a part of the excess reserves from the application of negative interest rates**. The idea is that a tiering system would allow the combination of (i) negative rates still effective at the margin and therefore passed on to money and capital markets, and (ii) the exemption of parts of the excess reserves moderating negative effects on bank profitability that could weaken the effectiveness of NIRP. By disconnecting the two, the transmission of NIRP to bank lending rates could be improved, and the "effective" lower bound, at which further rate cuts are no longer effective in terms of reducing bank lending rates, could be lowered. Still, reserve tiering does not fully eliminate the effects of negative interest rates on bank profitability. One source of bank profitability is the spread between interest rates on sight deposits of banks and interest rates on loans to non-banks, which are of longer duration. As the former turned out to be far less sensitive to NIRP than the latter, the spread between the two declined. Actually this effect is however not specific to NIRP, but also occurs to some extent with low (positive) interest rate policies.

4.2.2 Criticism of the Negative Interest Rate Policy

4.2.2.1 Financial Market Functioning Under Negative Interest Rates

Before the introduction of negative rates, there were some fears over whether money and other key financial markets can function at all with negative interest rates. As also noted by Bech and Malkhozov (2016, 37), steering short term interest rates into negative territory has not been particularly challenging, nor did financial markets change their behaviour in negative territory. One may add that the combination of NIRP and asset purchase programmes also pushed longer term bond yields into negative territory, e.g. for Switzerland, Japan and Germany for the entire risk-free yield curve, even beyond 10 years. Again, there was no indication of negative effects on market functioning.

4.2.2.2   General Counterproductive Effects
of Low/Negative Interest Rates

Finally, a number of critical authors have argued that central banks' low (and by implication, also negative) interest rate policies are ineffective or, at the very least, have major negative side effects that central banks tend to underestimate. These authors also seem to suggest that acknowledging the problem of low interest rate policies could lead to the conclusion that central banks should increase nominal interest rates without delay. The main arguments are as follows.

- Low interest rates would **weaken the life-time income prospects of savers**, and therefore lead to more saving and less consumption, and this would be negative for aggregate demand.
- Low interest rates would **create bubbles and therefore contribute to creating the next crisis** and undermining the efficiency of resource allocation.
- Low interest rates and elastic central bank liquidity supply weaken hard budget constraints because of their supportive effect to funding market access for indebted companies, households and the state. They therefore would lead to **zombification and low growth**, creating a vicious circle.

Bindseil et al. (2015) and others discuss and refute these arguments. The European Systemic Risk Board (2016) and the BIS (2018) have prepared extensive studies on macroprudential issues related to low interest rates. Overall, it seems that problems arise if economic agents deny the new reality of low real and nominal interest rates, and therefore either continue making unsustainable return promises to investors, or try, through unsound risk taking, to generate returns that are unrealistic. Also, if agents did not see the low interest rate environment coming and therefore took positions (or run a business model) that in the low interest rate scenario undermine their solvency, a transition issue arises that needs to be addressed in a way that minimises damage for society while keeping in mind moral hazard issues.

In sum: **negative interest rates may be viewed as an obvious continuation of Wicksellian interest rate policies** when the neutral level of interest rates falls into negative territory, as has become more likely in an environment with low growth potential and high central bank credibility as inflation fighters. In this sense, NIRP could be classified as a conventional monetary policy approach, reducing the need for non-conventional policy measures in the narrow sense with their possible more problematic side effects (such as large-scale asset purchase programmes). That NIRP is effective has been demonstrated by its strong effects on both capital market rates and bank lending rates. At the same time, two lower bound problems have to be acknowledged, namely (i) the one where banknote demand would explode; (ii) the one in which bank profitability would be undermined in such a way that a further lowering of central bank interest rates no longer leads to decreases in bank lending rates, as partially observed in Switzerland. While the former is also determined by storage and insurance costs of banknotes, the latter also depends on the willingness and ability of banks to pass on negative rates to different types of depositors and the amount of excess reserves that banks hold with the central bank at negative interest rates. While the two lower bounds are partially linked (through the decision of banks on whether to pass on negative rates to depositors), they are not necessarily the same. Both lower bounds could be overcome through a discontinuation of banknotes and their full replacement by CBDC—which however is not considered for a number of reasons as banknotes still have specific advantages.

4.3 Non-Conventional Credit Operations

Central banks have taken a variety of measures during the crisis to make their open market operations more supportive. Some of these measures relate to the lender-of-last-resort (LOLR) function, but even those are relevant from the monetary policy perspective. If the zero-lower bound is binding, strengthening the LOLR implies a reduction of funding stress to banks, which reduces pressure on them to deleverage or to increase the role of expensive funding sources. The LOLR therefore contributes to maintain the readiness of banks to provide credit to the economy at a moderate mark up to short-term risk-free rates.

First, central banks have **lengthened the duration of their lending operations** to banks, with the ECB going as far as four-year credit operations. Banks may consider a sequence of short-term borrowings from the central bank as inferior, from a liquidity risk perspective, to one longer-term borrowing operation. Consider three reasons for this: (i) Banks could perceive as uncertain the conditions under which central banks will provide short-term funding in the future (rates, access conditions, etc.). (ii) Even if the central bank commits to keep conditions for short-term access stable, e.g. it commits to full allotment at a given rate for its short-term operations for the next twelve months, banks may, as a matter of principle, find revolving short-term central bank refinancing less certain than twelve-month refinancing. (iii) Banks may be subject to some liquidity regulation, which treats longer-term refinancing from the central bank more favourably.

Second, central banks have replaced auction procedures to allocate central bank credit with **'fixed rate full allotment' (FRFA) operations**. The ECB has done so in October 2008 and ever since then has applied this simpler allotment procedure, which has the following advantages.

- It is more automatic and simpler than variable-rate tenders. This is per se a positive feature, as automatism means simplicity and transparency and hence fewer potential mistakes by the central bank and the commercial banks.
- In a liquidity crisis, the reduction of banks' uncertainty about the results of the tender assuages liquidity risk.
- It makes it possible to avoid aggressive bidding via high rates as it may take place with variable-rate tenders, thereby avoiding high and volatile marginal interest rates, which could imply unintended signals.
- The central bank no longer needs to estimate which allotment amount would ensure that market rates remain close to target rates. Carrying out fixed-rate full

allotment tenders is almost equivalent to setting the standing facility rate at the level of the target rate, with the only difference that an open market operation is not continuously open.

Third, central banks have **widened the access of counterparties to their credit operations**. When interbank markets break down, then financial institutions without recourse to central bank credit are in trouble, as they can no longer manage their day-to-day funding needs through credit operations with banks and capital market access. Allowing direct central bank access makes them independent from the functioning of interbank and capital markets.

Fourth, central banks have introduced **"targeted" credit operations** which make favourable lending terms (or access in general) conditional on some desirable behaviour of banks, such as providing more lending to the real economy. The ECB has done this through its so-called TLTRO operations, the Bank of Japan through its "Loan support programme" (LSP) and the Bank of England through its "Funding for lending scheme" (FLS).

Fifth, central banks have started to provide **credit in foreign currency, notably in USD**. The ECB and the Bank of Japan have done so since the end of 2007, based on swap lines established between central banks (see e.g. Goldberg et al. 2010). If USD spot and swap markets are impaired, this ensures that banks have sufficient USD funding to meet their obligations in USD (see Sheets et al. 2018).

Finally, widening the central bank collateral set applicable to credit operations is both a monetary policy and a LOLR measure, and will be discussed in more detail in Chapter 6. However, as Bindseil (2013) argues, it is also an unconventional monetary policy measure as it supports the ability of banks to continue providing credit and lowers the intermediation spread between short-term risk-free rates and bank lending rates. At the ZLB, compressing this spread or at least counteracting its increase can be decisive in preventing the economy from gliding into a deflationary trap.

4.4 Outright Purchase Programmes

All major central banks at some stage of the crisis that started in August 2007 established outright purchase programs for financial assets. The following eight objectives of such measures can be identified. The effects (3), (4), (6) and (7) can also be partially achieved through credit operations, but as credit operations are temporary, they may give less confidence to banks that the measure and the effects will be permanent.

(1) Reducing long-term risk-free interest rates

The transmission of monetary policy takes place via longer term rates, as most economic decisions (e.g. building a house or a new factory) depend on longer term rates. Longer term rates can be decomposed into an average of expected short term rates, plus a term premium (according to the expectations hypothesis of the term structure of interest rates). If the zero lower bound constrains reductions in short-term interest rates, then the central bank may want to provide further accommodation by at least reducing term premia through purchases of long-term bonds. This argument has been key to the Fed and the Bank of England programs that started in 2009.

(2) Compress credit and liquidity spreads ("market maker of last resort")

In a financial crisis, risky assets' prices may be depressed due to **asset fire sales and the absence of opportunistic buyers (i.e. buyers who buy whenever they feel an asset has become cheap)**. Moreover, arbitrage between asset classes may no longer work because of high bid-ask spreads, liquidity and capital constraints, systemic uncertainty, and self-fulfilling fears. In such an environment, the central bank can through purchases support depressed assets prices directly ease funding costs and constraints. Of course, central banks should not lower spreads below an adequate risk premium. Assessing what is an appropriate spread is of course challenging, in particular during a crisis.

(3) Inject excess reserves to strengthen banks' liquidity buffers

Large scale outright purchase programmes push the banking system into a liquidity surplus position towards the central bank. This facilitates central bank liquidity management and the control of the overnight rate (which will be close to the deposit facility rate, or to the rate of remuneration of excess reserves). More importantly, a situation of general excess reserves may support financial stability as most banks will feel re-assured in their short-term liquidity position.

(4) Inject excess reserves to increase the money supply via the money multiplier

Excess reserves targets play a role in the "money supply" approach to monetary policy implementation, as promoted in the official communication of the **Bank of Japan** between 2001 and 2016. This approach seems to be in line with traditional monetarist thinking.

(5) Absorbing risks from banks' into the central bank balance sheet and easing capital constraints of banks

The central bank may reduce total risk in banks' balance sheets by buying risky assets from them. Therefore, if banks feel constrained in terms of economic or regulatory capital, outright purchases by central banks may attenuate these constrains and thereby support their lending behaviour and thereby ease monetary conditions. Taking credit risk into the central bank balance sheet, e.g. in the form of purchases of a corporate bond portfolios, implies the need for the central bank to develop relevant expertise on credit risk management for this asset class. Moreover, in case of debt restructurings, the central bank will have to vote in bond holder assemblies, i.e., contribute to decisions which are remote to its core functions, and which entail reputational risks.

(6) Substituting banks' illiquid with liquid assets to improve overall liquidity of banks

Purchasing illiquid assets outright improves liquidity of banks, particularly if these assets were previously not eligible as central bank collateral, or only at a high haircut.

(7) Directly supporting through primary market purchases the funding liquidity of banks and/or other firms

By purchasing in the primary market bonds from issuers (unsecured bank bonds, covered bank bonds, corporate bonds, etc.), the central bank supports directly the funding of these institutions. Central bank purchases of debt of non-financial corporates (NFC), if done in the primary market, directly refinance the real sector and thus can offset the unwillingness of banks to provide their usual lending and liquidity services.

(8) Threat to "purchase all real assets in the world" to counter perception of deflationary trap

Central banks are in principle able to purchase all assets of the world with the money that they can issue without constraints—in particular in a deflationary context. When central banks launch such potentially infinite purchase programs, the other economic agents will become less willing to sell all their assets (including equity, commodities, etc.), and they will thus require higher and higher prices, and hence the purchasing power of the currency will fall. In the case of a credible central bank, this will be anticipated, and the announcement of such a purchase program should immediately defeat deflation.

Impact of purchase programmes on yield levels

There is a growing empirical literature estimating the effects of large-scale asset purchase programmes on the risk-free yield curve and its further transmission to other interest rates and the real economy (a comprehensive recent study covering the programmes of the US, UK, Japan and the euro area is Agostini et al. 2016). Effects on long-term interest rates of recent large-scale asset purchase programmes are generally believed to be in the area of up to 100 basis points. In combination with NIRP, this would mean that these two policies together could achieve reductions of long-term funding rates of up to 200 basis points, which obviously means substantial further easing (NIRP also contributes to reduce long-term rates as expectations on future short-term interest rates decrease). When looking more precisely at the effects of purchase programmes on asset prices and long-term yields, it is important to distinguish between the following three effects (D'Amico and King 2011 were the first to investigate theoretical and empirical aspects of flow vs stock effects of the US Fed's asset purchase programmes):

- **Stock effect:** if there are static demand and supply elasticities for different types of securities (based on investors' static preferred habitats), then one would expect that the eventual stock of securities purchased in a programme will determine the price impact.
- **Flow effect:** if the price of an asset is driven essentially by the daily demand and supply conditions and if agents' ability to bridge prices across time through intertemporal arbitrage is limited, then the daily flows of purchases and sales would matter. The strength of flow effects of an asset purchase program will therefore depend on (i) the pace of purchases (purchased volume per unit of time); (ii) the efficiency and flexibility of market makers and investors to do intertemporal arbitrage and warehouse positions accordingly; (iii) the speed at

which investors are able or willing to adjust their stocks, which also depends on who in particular holds the assets (a pension fund vs a bank in its trading book); (iv) the time between the announcement of the programme and its start (more time allows investors to prepare for selling assets and dealers to accumulate stocks waiting for the central bank).

- **Announcement effect**: if asset prices in principle reflect at any moment in time all available information, it can be expected that most of the impact on prices and yields materialises immediately when the central bank announces an asset purchase program. The announcement effect should be an anticipation of the stock effect, and not of the flow effect. The announcement effect will mainly depend on (i) the degree to which the announcement has not been anticipated (for example, when the ECB's PSPP was announced, markets hardly moved as it had been anticipated); (ii) the credibility of the central bank (determined, for example, by its history of meticulously implementing what it promises); (iii) how remote in the future the promised measures are (with non-perfect central bank credibility, more remote measures will have a lesser announcement effect than measures which are relatively nearby), (iv) the clarity of the announcement.

Central bank purchases with too short lead times (after the program's announcement) and at a too high pace distorts markets, in the sense of letting yields temporarily undershoot more than necessary. It also implies that the central bank will over-pay. Buying with too long lead times and with a too low pace unnecessarily delays the desired easing of financial conditions. Interestingly, in the case of limited central bank credibility, stronger flow effects may be desirable as they contribute to a quick price adjustment, i.e. a faster effectiveness of monetary easing, without this implying that the central bank purchases at excessive prices. A less credible central bank should therefore buy at a higher pace and start faster than a credible central bank, which can immediately achieve stock effects.

4.5   Distinguishing Between Conventional, Non-Conventional, and LOLR Policies

Central banks have, despite the presumption that non-conventional measures have negative side effects and conventional measures have not, maintained non-standard measures beyond what is strictly implied by the existence of the ZLB: For example, the Fed's policy normalisation has consisted first in withdrawing accommodation through a number of standard interest rate increases, before reducing its stock of LSAP-securities. This was explained to be preferable because rate hikes would be easier to dose than the impact of changes of securities stocks on the stance of monetary policy. Moreover, it would be easier to switch direction by changes of interest rates than in terms of changes to a securities stock. Also, in 2007 and 2008 central banks undertook various non-standard measures without having yet reached the zero lower bound. Those may have related to LOLR measures, which may be beneficial for society regardless of having reached the ZLB or not (because the LOLR may save viable and solvent, but temporarily illiquid projects).

While the LOLR will only be discussed in Chapter 6, it is interesting here to try to put order into the three types of policy objectives determining the specification of central bank market operations. The following chart puts the LOLR into context with conventional and non-conventional monetary policies and assigns central bank financial operations and instruments to any of the three (overlapping) areas (Fig. 4.1).

- **Control of short-term interest rates** is the classical form of conventional monetary policy.
- **NIRP (negative interest rate policy)** can be classified as "conventional" monetary policy, as it is in some way just a continuation of central bank short-term interest rate policies. Still, it has something unconventional, as it had never been done before 2013.
- **TLTRO (targeted longer-term refinancing operations) and QE ("quantitative easing") types of asset purchase programs** are pure non-conventional monetary policy operations.

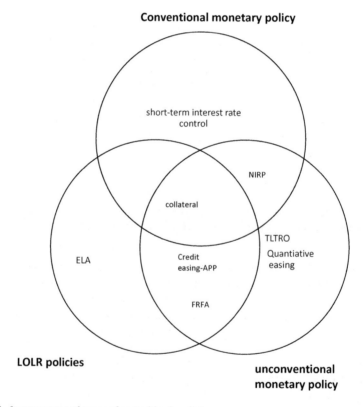

Fig. 4.1 Instruments and types of central bank policies

- **Credit easing asset purchase programs** are unconventional monetary policy measures but can also have LOLR content, if the program aims (also) at improving the funding liquidity of the firms issuing the debt purchased.
- **FRFA (Fixed rate full allotment) credit operations** attenuate funding fears of banks, and in this sense are a LOLR measure. At the same time, they support the willingness of banks to provide credit to the real economy, which at the zero-lower bound adds policy accommodation.
- **ELA (Emergency liquidity assistance)** is by definition outside monetary policy. At the same time, ELA may prevent contagion of a narrow liquidity issue to the rest of the financial system, which would have repercussions for monetary policy transmission. In this sense, ELA decisions may often be non-neutral for monetary policy.
- **Collateral** is the one and only element in the intersection of the three circles: it is necessary to conventional monetary policy credit operations, and in exceptional circumstances (liquidity crises and/or zero-lower bound problem), broadening the collateral set supports funding liquidity of banks, which attenuates the crisis and supports bank lending.

Chapter 5
Financial Instability

5.1 Liquidity, Asset Prices, and Default

Financial crises always encompass liquidity crisis, and liquidity crises typically have a funding liquidity and a market liquidity component. In a *funding* **liquidity crisis**, the problem is credit availability: debtors cannot obtain credit to roll over their liabilities, as money and capital markets freeze. In a *market* **liquidity crisis**, bid-ask spreads and asset fire-sale discounts increase, reducing the total liquidity obtainable through asset liquidation.

Liquidity crises may lead to the inability of debtors to fulfil their contractual obligations and hence to their default, with additional economic damage. Financial crises are typically triggered by **strong downward revisions of asset values** (Bagehot 1873, Kindleberger and Aliber 2011). Asset price changes can be driven by any major unexpected news the economy, e.g. a natural disaster, a pandemic, an unexpected change of government and of economic policies, the outbreak of a war, the rise of a new major technology, a strong re-assessment of the inflation and thus central bank interest rate outlook, a strong collective re-assessment of the prospects of an asset class (e.g. burst of a housing bubble) etc. can all heavily impact on few, or various asset classes. For example, the outbreak of Covid-19 and the uncertain perspective of a return to the pre-Covid19 normal has reduced the value of assets owned by the international travel and tourist industry (cruise ships, airplanes, hotels, etc.).

Strong declines of asset values have various negative effects on economic agents. Solvency declines, which undermines the ability to access funding sources and the willingness and the ability to undertake risky projects. In the case of banks, a decline in solvency puts at risk compliance with capital adequacy regulations, adding urgency to deleveraging through the shrinking of lending or through asset fire sales. In the case of households, lower wealth reduces consumption, which will have recessionary effects.

© The Author(s) 2021   67
U. Bindseil and A. Fotia, *Introduction to Central Banking*,
SpringerBriefs in Quantitative Finance,
https://doi.org/10.1007/978-3-030-70884-9_5

Table 5.1 Balance sheet of an indebted firm

Assets		Liabilities	
Assets	$A + \varepsilon$	Debt	D
		Equity	$E + \varepsilon$

The mechanisms of liquidity crises have been similar across time. Already Thornton (1802) noticed the problem of liquidity hoarding and bank runs, and how they relate to a lack of trust.

Bagehot (1873, Chapter VI "Why Lombard Street Is Often Very Dull, and Sometimes Extremely Excited") argues that while liquidity crises are caused by heterogenous exogenous events, their mechanics, once having been triggered, are similar:

> Any sudden event which creates a great demand for actual cash may cause, and will tend to cause, a panic in a country where cash is much economised, and where debts payable on demand are large. .... Such accidental events are of the most various nature: a bad harvest, an apprehension of foreign invasion, the sudden failure of a great firm which everybody trusted, and many other similar events, have all caused a sudden demand for cash. And some writers have endeavoured to classify panics according to the nature of the particular accidents producing them. But little, however, is, I believe, to be gained by such classifications. There is little difference in the effect of one accident and another upon our credit system. We must be prepared for all of them, and we must prepare for all of them in the same way—by keeping a large cash reserve.

Understanding the logic of liquidity crises is a precondition for understanding the role of the central bank in stopping the escalation of liquidity crises and in addressing their economic consequences.

To illustrate how default probabilities increase in financial crises when assets values decline, consider in **Table** 5.1 the balance sheet of a leveraged financial or non-financial corporate with ε being a random variable impacting asset values.

Asset values can be thought of as being subject to periodic random shocks ε. Assuming simplistically that ε is N(0, σ_ε) **then the probability of default (PD)** of a company, in the sense of the probability that its asset values will fall below the value of debt in the next time period, could be estimated as ($\Phi(\cdot)$ is the cumulative standard normal distribution):

$$PD = P(E + \varepsilon < 0) = P(A + \varepsilon < D) = \Phi\left(-\frac{A - D}{\sigma_\varepsilon}\right)$$

This formula for the probability of default is however a strong simplification, since asset values are not normally distributed, variables such as σ_ε are not directly observable, time is continuous, and there is no unique horizon to consider. Moreover, default does not need to occur exactly when $A + \varepsilon$ touches D, since default is eventually triggered by illiquidity. Merton's structural credit model (Merton 1974) is a more sophisticated version of this basic default probability model.

Table 5.2 Annual default probability of rated debtors according to Standard and Poor's S&P 2020

Annual default rates	AAA	AA	A	BBB	BB	B	CCC/C
Minimum	0.00	0.00	0.00	0.00	0.00	0.25	0.00
Maximum	0.00	0.38	0.39	1.02	4.24	13.84	49.46
Weighted average	0.00	0.02	0.05	0.16	0.61	3.33	27.08

Rating agencies provide comprehensive statistics on how rated debtors performed. For example, Standard & Poor's regularly publishes a statistical default study (e.g. S&P 2020). According to **Table** 5.2, the following annual default rates applied in the period 1981 to 2019.

The differences between good years (minimum) and bad years (maximum) are significant. The time series of annual default shows a sort of financial cycle with peaks in default frequency around 1991, 2001, and 2008. Creditors do not only care about the **probability of default**, but also about **what losses occur in case of default**. If all debtors rank pari passu, and if default occurs exactly when $A + \varepsilon = D$, then the "Loss-given default" (LGD, $= 1 -$ recovery ratio) should be zero (the recovery ratio should be 1). However, evidence collected by rating agencies suggests that LGDs are on average around 50% (depending also on the debt instrument). This can have two explanations: (i) default often occurs only when A is already clearly below D (i.e. creditors did not realize that the company had negative equity, or there was no debt redemption date); (ii) the default event itself is costly, as default implies that organisational and human capital is destroyed and specific assets are liquidated at fire-sale prices (e.g. a sophisticated machine is sold at its raw material value, minus the costs of removing, transporting and dismantling the machine).

The corporate finance literature provides estimates of the costs of default between 10 and 44% (e.g. Glover 2016; Davydenko et al. 2012). The cost of default is one key reason for **central banks trying to prevent defaults of sound companies due to illiquidity**. We will see below that in settings of asymmetric information which are typical for the high uncertainty prevailing in financial crisis, credit and asset markets can break down such that illiquidity and default can occur even for firms which are solvent and viable.

The "credit channel" literature has analysed since the 1980s how high credit riskiness and low equity have been identified for a while as an issue for monetary policy transmission. According to this literature, low equity implies higher agency costs in the lending between banks and corporates. Lower bank equity implies higher agency costs between holders of bank liabilities and banks. Higher agency costs result from a deterioration of the alignment of incentives between debt and equity owners when equity levels fall (e.g. Holmström and Tirole 1997). In addition, debtors with insufficient equity will attempt to restore their creditworthiness by aiming at deleveraging, causing economic contraction and deflationary tendencies.

To sum up, it is important to distinguish the following four key concepts for troubled debtor:

- **defaulted**: a missed payment obligation, possibly defined also by the number of days the payment day passed;
- **illiquid**: inability to identify money for fulfilling (forthcoming) payment obligations;
- **insolvent**: debt exceeds assets, and therefore equity is negative;
- **over-indebtedness**: Relating to insolvency but less linked to a strict threshold. Overindebted companies may still have positive capital, but insufficient capital to grant them healthy and sufficiently cheap market access, so that in the medium-term insolvency/illiquidity looms.

An indebted corporate can default despite being solvent. It may be illiquid because a systemic liquidity crisis situation made all possible lenders stop lending, and it has to refinance a maturing loan or debt instrument. A corporate may be insolvent without yet defaulting, because no debt payment is due. Eventually, a corporate which is clearly insolvent will also end up being illiquid and default because it does not make sense for creditors to give fresh loans to an insolvent debtor.

5.2   Conditional and Unconditional Insolvency, and Bank Runs

Debtors that are **solvent conditional on the access to funding** may become insolvent if funding constraints force them to undertake fire sales of some of their assets at some specified horizon. This relates to problems explained in Sect. 1.2 that fair book values of assets are normally higher than their (short-term) liquidation value. The following assumes that the fair value of the assets of an indebted company is 1, and that these assets are ordered from the most liquid to the least liquid (x-axis). Assume further that $L(x)$ is the liquidity generated by liquidating at some time horizon, say one week, the share x of assets that is most liquid. It follows that $L(0) = 0$ (if no assets are sold, no liquidity is generated), $L(1) \leq 1$ (a sale of all assets provides at the very maximum their book value), $dL(x)/dx \geq 0$ (the liquidity generated cannot decrease with more assets being sold) and $d^2L(x)/d^2x \leq 0$ (each new unit of asset sold does not provide more liquidity than the previous one, as assets were ranked from the most to the least liquid). In other words, the liquidity generation can be described by a concave monotonously non-decreasing function of x. We can also define similarly the fire-sale loss function $F(x) = x - L(x)$ which indicates the fire-sale losses generated by selling a share of assets x, starting with the most liquid assets. The function $f(x) = dF(x)/dx$ is the marginal fire-sales loss function indicating the size of fire-sale losses resulting from selling the asset ranked at x, and $q(x) = dL(x)/dx = 1 - f(x)$ is the marginal liquidity generated by selling the asset ranked x.

Figure 5.1 illustrates the **simple case when $f(x) = x$, and therefore $q(x) = 1 - x$, $F(x) = x^2/2$ and $L(x) = x - x^2/2$.** For example, if the company needs to generate a liquidity of L_1 in order to meet a due payment to its bondholders, then it needs to solve the quadratic equation $L_1 = x - x^2/2$ or $x^2/2 - x + L_1 = 0$. The relevant solution to this problem is $x = 1 - (\sqrt{1 - 2L_1})$. For example, if $L_1 = 0.4$, then the required

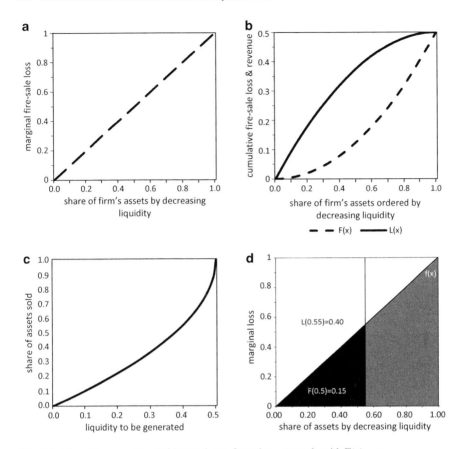

Fig. 5.1 Liquidity generation and losses due to fire sales—example with F(x) = x

fire sales are x = 0.55. **Figure** 5.1a draws the marginal fire sale loss function f(x) for the assets x ordered from the most liquid to the least liquid. **Figure** 5.1b shows the total fire-sale loss F(x) and total liquidity generated L(x) for f(x) = x, again for liquidity-ordered assets. **Figure** 5.1c shows the necessary fire sales of assets as a function of the liquidity to be generated, i.e. x = L^{-1}(L$_1$). Last but not least, **Fig.** 5.1d illustrates the concrete case when the firm needs to generate the cash flow of 0.4, whereby a share of 0.55 of the assets need to be sold.

Assume the company has equity E, and has to generate through fire sales a cash flow at a certain time horizon T. For instance, because it needs to repay a debt instrument at maturity and is unable to roll it over or find another form of financing. For every time horizon T the function L$_T$(x) is non-decreasing and therefore invertible, so that we can write the inverse function x$_T$(L), describing the share of assets that must be liquidated for generating liquidity of a specified size L. Then, the company is solvent conditional on the need to generate a cash flow L_1 at time horizon $T = 1$ if, and only if, the fire-sales losses caused by the liquidation are lower than the equity of the company:

$$F_1(x_1(L_1)) < E$$

We expect that the higher the time horizon, the lower the losses: if $T_1 > T_2$, then for every x, we expect that $f_{T2}(x) \geq f_{T1}(x)$. To distinguish fire-sale losses due to time constraints from fire-sale losses due to asset specificity, one could say that the marginal fire-sale losses **due to asset specificity** (f_{AS}) are the marginal fire-sale losses without any time pressure, i.e.

$$f_{AS}(x) = \lim_{T \to \infty} f_T(x)$$

Consequently, the marginal fire-sale losses due **exclusively to time pressure** ($f_{T,P}$) can be defined as the difference between the marginal loss function and the asset-specificity related marginal loss function.

$$f_{T,P}(x) = f_T(x) - f_{AS}(x)$$

Figure 5.2 provides an example of marginal fire sale loss functions for the same company at different time horizons.

Fig. 5.2 Marginal fire sales loss curve for alternative liquidation horizons

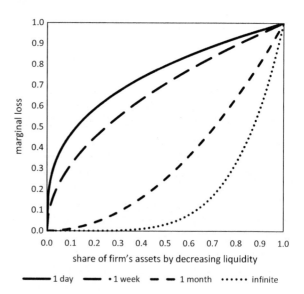

To ensure funding stability, the bank (or any debtor) should ideally be able to ensure liquidity and solvency at all time horizons. For example, if one debt position of an amount L_1 matures in 1 week, and another of L_2 in four weeks, then both conditions

$$F_{1\text{Week}}(x_{1\text{Week}}(L_1)) \; < \; E \text{ and } F_{4\text{Weeks}}(x_{4\text{Weeks}}(L_1 + L_2)) \; < \; E$$

should be fulfilled in order to ensure that the debtor is stable and can communicate to its current or potential future creditors that it will be fine anyway (even conditional on no roll-over of funding). Chapter 6 will provide a more precise model in which, for a specific functional form of $L(x)$ and $F(x)$, precise conditions for funding stability will be derived.

For the moment, it is useful to retain that (i) solvent debtors can be sub-classified into those which are solvent regardless of assumptions taken with regards their ability to roll over some debt instruments maturing at some horizon, and those which are solvent only conditional on accessing fresh funding; (ii) the latter may create multiple equilibrium situations, as further explained in chapter 6; (iii) both a negative asset value and a deterioration of asset liquidity can push a lender from being unconditionally solvent into being solvent only subject to funding renewal.

Bank runs have been a major issue at least since the nineteenth century, with particularly devastating episodes in the early 1930s, leading to the general introduction of deposit insurance schemes. More recent runs occurred in the UK (Northern Rock in 2008), and in Greece and Cyprus during the euro sovereign debt crisis. The latter runs mainly materialised through electronic transfers of deposits to accounts with non-domestic euro area banks, i.e. without queues in front of the banks to withdraw cash. Bank runs have been extensively modelled in the economic literature, such as in Diamond and Dybvig (1983) and Rochet and Vives (2004). The particularity of bank runs is their self-fulfilling property: once a run on a bank starts, it can lead to the default of the bank, confirming the individual wisdom of those who were first in the queue to withdraw their money. We will illustrate in chapter 7, with a very simple but powerful strategic bank run model, that a bank can essentially be in three states in terms of stability of its short-term liabilities:

(a) **Funding stability**: if there is a single no-run equilibrium. This should apply for unconditionally solvent banks.

(b) **Multiple equilibria**: there are two equilibria, one in which depositors run, and one in which they do not run. The depositors' behaviour can in principle switch from one to the other. This situation arises for solvent banks which are however conditionally insolvent, i.e. conditionally on a run.

(c) **Single run equilibrium**: depositors and other short-term investors will run in any case when a bank is unconditionally insolvent.

A switch from state a) to state b) can occur if: (i) asset liquidity deteriorates; and/or (ii) asset values decline, implying a decline of equity. A switch from state a) or b) to state c) will occur if asset values fall such that equity becomes negative. In crisis situations, both factors tend to materialise with higher probability than usual, in particular for banks with more limited solvency and liquidity buffers, or with an unlucky asset concentration, i.e. an asset concentration towards those assets which by bad luck suffer from value losses and a decline in liquidity. This will be taken up in chapter 6 and in particular in the model of Sect. 6.5.

5.3 Illiquidity in Credit and Dealer Markets

In this section we attempt to shed further light on the mechanisms leading to illiquidity in credit and asset markets.

5.3.1 Credit Markets

Information asymmetries can lead to a freeze of credit markets and related economic damage (e.g. Stiglitz and Weiss 1981; Bolton and Freixas 2006). The following basic model of a credit market freeze is based on Flannery (1996). It is assumed that entrepreneurs who would like to borrow are either "Good" or "Bad", i.e., will repay or not, respectively. The proportion of Good entrepreneurs is g, while the proportion of Bad entrepreneurs is $(1 - g)$. The entrepreneur needs a unit bank loan to finance her project. At the end of the period, Good entrepreneurs' projects will be worth $V_G > 1$, which suffices to repay loans, assuming that the lending interest rate was not higher than $V_G - 1$.

Banks are imperfect in assessing loan applicants. The creditworthiness will be assessed correctly with a probability p. The bank obtains either a signal, S_G (good borrower) or a signal S_B (bad borrower). If the borrower is actually good, then with probability $p > g$, a good borrower signal (S_G) is captured, and the bank may lend. With probability $(1 - p)$, the bad borrower signal (S_B) is received, and no loan will be provided. If the borrower is actually bad, then the bad borrower signal will be received by the bank with probability p, and the good borrower signal with probability $(1 - p)$. With the help of Bayes' Law (shown below explicitly only for the first of the four cases), this allows the calculation of the probabilities of all combinations of signal and actual quality of entrepreneurs:

$$P(S_G|G) = \frac{P(S_G \cap G)}{P(G)} \Rightarrow P(S_G \cap G) = pg$$

$$P(S_B|B) = p(1 - g)$$

$$P(S_G|B) = (1 - p)(1 - g); \ P(S_B|G) = (1 - p)g$$

Banks are assumed to be competitive and to have zero profits, implying that **profits from lending to good borrowers must on average compensate the credit losses due to bad borrowers**. Let j* be the interest rate that a bank needs to set to have zero expected profits. As lending occurs only if a good signal is obtained, non-zero pay offs occur only in two out of the four possible cases. The zero-profit condition can therefore be formulated as follows for a bank that itself pays zero interest on its liabilities:

$$j^* \cdot gp + (-1)(1 - g)(1 - p) = 0$$

$$\Rightarrow j^* = \frac{(1 - g)(1 - p)}{gp}$$

Lending, i.e., an active credit market, will take place as long as $V_G - 1 \geq j^*$. Otherwise, even good entrepreneurs would make losses and will therefore better not launch their projects. For example, writing j* as j*(g,p): j*(0.5, 0.5) = 100%, j*(0.5, 0.75) = 33%; j*(0.5, 0.9) = 11%; j*(0.7, 0.9) = 4.8%, etc.

The model illustrates three causes for a break-down of credit markets: first, a decline of g, the share of Good entrepreneurs; second, a decrease of V_G, the project return of Good entrepreneurs; third, a decrease of p, the power of the banks' screening technology. All three effects are associated with a negative economic shock. The model thereby explains why economic shocks trigger credit market crises, and moreover why these effects can be so abrupt: according to the model, a minor further parameter deterioration can make the market collapse, because the critical condition no longer holds. But even before such a complete funding market breakdown, economic deterioration is already felt in the form of an increasing equilibrium lending rate j*. This matters at the zero lower bound, when the central bank can no longer compensate such effects through a lowering of its interest rates.

5.3.2 Dealer Markets

Assume a dealer market in which dealers commit bid and ask prices for some standard quantity q. The bid-ask spread, which measures asset liquidity, typically increases in financial crises. The following simple model takes up basic elements of Kyle (1985) to explain why asset liquidity in a dealer market will deteriorate in a financial crisis. The model assumes that:

- the **fair value of the asset, A_t**, changes every day according to $A_t = A_{t-1} + \varepsilon_t$ with ε_t being a symmetric random variable with expected value 0.

- Every morning, the **market maker** sets the **bid-ask spread** z around his estimate of A_t, which is however A_{t-1}, as he learns about ε_t only with a one day lag. Therefore the bid and ask price set by the market maker are $A_{t-1} - z/2$ and $A_{t-1} + z/2$, respectively. Market makers are assumed to provide their services under full competition and to not have operating costs.
- **Noise traders** are uninformed market participants which trade every day an amount W, equally split between demand and supply. The amount W declines when the bid-ask spread increases (dW/dz < 0).
- Only the **insider** knows ε_t and thus A_t on day t. Whenever A_t is outside the bid-ask spread, i.e. whenever $A_t < A_{t-1} - z/2$ or $A_t > A_{t-1} + z/2$, the insider exploits the commitment of the market maker and deals with him. The market maker is assumed to become aware of an insider transaction only once he notes the imbalance in demand and supply has reached q. Then, and assuming that the noise-traders have achieved W(z), the market maker stops quoting for that day and only re-opens t + 1 with a bid-ask spread around A_t.

Bid-ask spreads and trading volumes will reflect the existence of insider information, as captured by σ_ε^2. The competitive market maker will set z such that expected profits are zero. Expected profits have two components: the profit of market makers generated by the noise traders is z·W(z). If $f_\varepsilon(x)$ is the density function of asset value innovations ε_t, then the expected losses of the market maker due to insiders are:

$$\left[\int_{-\infty}^{-\frac{z}{2}} \left(x + \frac{z}{2} \right) f_\varepsilon(x)dx + \int_{\frac{z}{2}}^{\infty} \left(x - \frac{z}{2} \right) f_\varepsilon(x)dx \right] q$$

The competitive equilibrium bid-ask spread z is the one in which the expected profits of the market maker are zero, with the profits extracted from noise traders compensating exactly the expected losses due to insiders. The model illustrates the empirical pattern that information intensity and price volatility of assets reduce asset liquidity, as measured by bid-ask spread, for example. It thereby also explains the strong increases of bid-ask spreads in financial crises, which tend to be characterised by an intensive news flow and high uncertainty.

5.4 Increasing Haircuts and Margin Calls

Financial exposures are often protected by collateral, also called "margin", such as in particular in the following three cases: (i) Interbank repo operations (i.e. collateralised interbank lending); (ii) Lending of banks to non-banks: e.g. mortgage loans; loans of banks to corporates, to hedge funds, etc. (iii) derivatives transactions, be they via central clearing counterparties (CCPs), or "over-the counter" (OTC), i.e. directly between counterparties.

The **unexpected request of large amounts of additional collateral ("margining")** can trigger liquidity crises and depreciate asset values via forced fire sales because margin requirements limit leverage for investors that use as collateral the assets they invest in. Large marginal calls of counterparties were the eventual trigger of the defaults of Lehman brothers in September 2008. Margin calls of CCPs in March 2020 related to the outbreak of the Covid-19 pandemic also created significant stress on banks, but remained manageable (see Huang and Takats 2020).

In financial crises, margin requirements tend to increase substantially. If the cash investor (or a CCP) wants to maintain the probability of a loss conditional on counterparty default at a certain confidence level, then it needs to increase haircuts whenever volatility increases, liquidity decreases, or the desired protection level increases. Haircuts are often set such as to limit the probability of a loss at a certain confidence level in the scenario of collateral liquidation due to borrower default. **The haircut is thus calculated on the basis of the following factors:**

- The assumed orderly liquidation time T of the asset, i.e. the liquidation time such that liquidation does not negatively affect market prices.
- The asset price volatility σ at a one-day horizon. If daily price changes are independent of each other, then volatility of price changes over T will be $\sigma\sqrt{T}$.
- The confidence level for not making a loss. For normally distributed price changes, the confidence level β can be translated into a multiplier of volatility using the inverted cumulative standard normal distribution, i.e. $\Phi^{-1}(\beta)$.

We obtain therefore the following adequate haircut h for a daily price volatility σ, a liquidation horizon of T days, and a confidence level β to avoid a loss in case counterparty default and collateral liquidation:

$$h = \Phi^{-1}(\beta)\sigma\sqrt{T}$$

In a financial crisis, haircuts will increase because (i) cash providers may seek a higher confidence level of protection as their capital buffers may have suffered due to the crisis, implying a need to reduce overall risk taking: $\beta \uparrow \Rightarrow \Phi^{-1}(\beta) \uparrow$; (ii) asset price volatility increases: $\sigma \uparrow$; (iii) it takes longer to liquidate assets without the liquidation having additional price effects: $T\uparrow$. Increases in haircuts will mean less leverage, and thus, for a given level of capital, the need for fire sales with various potential second round effects.

5.5 Interaction Between Crisis Channels

The various crisis channels described in this chapter interact and create vicious circles of deteriorating solvency, liquidity and default leading potentially to an economic meltdown:

- Asset value declines **may lead to immediate insolvency**, which normally will lead to an inability to roll over funding, and eventual default.

- Even if immediate insolvency can be avoided, still **various liquidity channels set in**, like loss of funding stability, increasing funding costs due to increased credit risk premia, increase of haircuts, increase of bid-ask spreads, and decline in the ability to monitor and to overcome the adverse selection problem (all illustrated above in simple models).
- Banks' and corporates' funding stress possibly forces them to undertake **asset fire sales**.
- These fire sales may prevent the immediate default of the bank or corporate. Nevertheless, the firm can have generated losses through fire sales that depleted its equity.
- Defaults and fire sales create **further asset value declines and a further increase of asset value uncertainty**.

Once lending to the real economy tightens, a recession can occur and will lead to additional losses via renewed asset price declines and impairment of banks' loan portfolios. The resulting dynamics may call for external circuit breakers, including in particular the central bank. Central banks are not subject to liquidity constraints and can in theory provide unlimited liquidity to banks. Thereby, they can suppress the liquidity part of any vicious crisis circle, making the central bank (unwillingly) the key player deciding on the fate of banks and other leveraged entities.

Chapter 6
The Central Bank as Lender of Last Resort

In this chapter we review the function of the central bank as lender of last resort (LOLR), starting from the understanding of financial crises developed in the previous chapter. We recall long-established LOLR principles: proactive lending, inertia of the central bank risk control framework, and risk endogeneity. Because of its systemic role, a central bank should not tighten its collateral framework in a crisis, as restrictive policies are likely to not only increase the overall damage done by a crisis to society, but to even increase central bank losses. We explain in more detail the main reasons why a central bank should act as LOLR: prevent negative externalities from fire sales; its unique status as institution with unlimited liquidity; its status as a risk-free counterparty making others accept to deliver collateral to it even at high haircuts; and its mandate to preserve price stability. We distinguish three different forms of LOLR: elements built into the regular operational framework; readiness to relax parameters in a crisis; and provision of emergency liquidity assistance to individual firms. We then discuss what could be the optimal propensity of a central bank to engage in LOLR activities and outline possible trade-offs. Last but not least, we develop a bank-run model which highlights the role of asset liquidity and central bank eligible collateral. We calculate through a model variant with binary asset liquidity and uniform central bank collateral haircut, but then also introduce a model variant with continuous asset liquidity and haircuts.

© The Author(s) 2021
U. Bindseil and A. Fotia, *Introduction to Central Banking*,
SpringerBriefs in Quantitative Finance,
https://doi.org/10.1007/978-3-030-70884-9_6

6.1 Principles and Rationale for the Central Bank Acting as Lender of Last Resort

6.1.1 Origin and Principles of LOLR

While large-scale and successful LOLR measures of central banks can be traced back to at least 1763 (e.g. Bindseil 2019), today's thinking on the LOLR function is still strongly inspired by nineteenth century experience, and in particular Walter Bagehot's *Lombard Street* of 1873 (see also e.g. Goodhart 1999; Goodhart and Illing 2002). Consider three key insights of nineteenth century experience which still appear valid today.

Lend pro-actively while preserving the safety of the central bank. In a hearing of the Lords' Committee in 1832, Bank of England director Jeremiah Harman summarised the Bank's actions in the panic of 1825 as follows (see Bagehot 1873):

> We lent… by every possible means, and in modes that we never had adopted before; we took in stock of security, we purchased Exchequer bills, we made advances on Exchequer bills, we not only discounted outright, but we made advances on deposits of bills to an immense amount; in short, by every possible means consistent with the safety of the Bank;… seeing the dreadful state in which the public were, we rendered every assistance in our power.

Harman presents the Bank of England's action as having been *creative and pro-active*, i.e. to have innovated to find the best ways to support funding liquidity of financial institutions, the only constraint to creativity being the need to preserve the "safety of the Bank", i.e. limit additional risk taking.

Inertia of risk control framework. Bagehot (1873) himself advises the Bank of England that, in a crisis, it should maintain its risk control framework broadly unchanged, and not tighten it similarly to private lenders as a reaction to a worsened asset quality and liquidity, as well as higher volatility, etc.:

> If it is known that the Bank of England is freely advancing on what in ordinary times is reckoned a good security and on what is then commonly pledged and easily convertible, the alarm of the solvent merchants and bankers will be stayed. But if securities, really good and usually convertible, are refused by the Bank, the alarm will not abate, the other loans made will fail in obtaining their end, and the panic will become worse and worse.

Bagehot refers to various episodes in which the Bank of England did not follow this principle and ended up making the crisis worse than it would have needed to be.

Risk Endogeneity. Bagehot argues that supportive liquidity provision could be necessary *to minimize* the Bank of England's eventual own financial risks, because it would be the only way to prevent a financial meltdown with unavoidable large losses also for the Bank of England:

(M)aking no loans as we have seen will ruin it (Bank of England); making large loans and stopping, as we have also seen, will ruin it. The only safe plan for the Bank is the brave plan, to lend in a panic on every kind of current security, or every sort on which money is ordinarily and usually lent. This policy may not save the Bank; but if it does not, nothing will save it.

In other words, the riskiness of exposures would itself be endogenous to the central bank measures. Liberal central bank lending could imply lower central bank financial risk taking than tight risk controls, turning upside down the logic of private lenders.

6.1.2 Why Should Central Banks Be Lenders of Last Resort?

We identify five reasons for a central bank to act as lender of last resort in a financial crisis.

6.1.2.1 Negative Externalities of Funding Liquidity Stress

Public authorities may intervene in markets in case of negative externalities. A major negative externality of bank stress relates to the fire sale spiral induced by liquidity problems of individual banks. If banks are forced to sell assets to generate liquidity, these sales likely depress market prices. In turn, this generates renewed solvency and liquidity stress for banks, possibly triggering further fire sales, etc. Central bank loans which reduce the need for asset fire sales can prevent such a downward spiral. Asset fire sales are not the only form of negative externalities of bank funding stress and illiquidity-induced default. Other negative externalities are, for example, the contagion of depositors' fears if they observe a bank run, possibly leading to further bank runs such as observed in the early 1930s.

6.1.2.2 Central Banks Have Unlimited Liquidity (in a Paper Standard)

Unlike leveraged private entities, a central bank is not threatened by illiquidity in the currency it issues. Modern central banks are endowed with the monopoly and freedom to issue legal tender. It is therefore opportune that, in case of a liquidity crisis when all financial and non-financial institution tend to hoard liquidity, central banks remain willing to lend and to hold illiquid assets outright or as collateral. This is unrelated to negative externalities, and even if a central bank were purely profit-oriented, its unique access to liquidity justifies lending and purchases of illiquid assets in a crisis.

6.1.2.3   Haircuts Are a Particularly Effective Risk Mitigation Tool for Central Banks

Haircuts are an effective tool if the collateral provider is more credit risky than the cash investor. In contrast, haircuts are less effective if cash provider and collateral provider are equally credit risky since the implied protection of the cash provider is at the expense of the collateral provider (Ewerhart and Tapking 2008). Therefore, simply increasing haircuts in symmetric interbank repo markets is not an adequate solution to provide more risk protection, while it is for asymmetric relationships, such as the one between a prime bank lending to a hedge fund. From the perspective of the collateral provider, a central bank is a risk-free counterparty as it cannot default and will always return pledged collateral. Central bank credit against illiquid collateral can be well-protected through high haircuts, without the collateral provider feeling unduly exposed. Against any other cash provider, i.e. against any credit risky cash provider, the collateral provider would likely be unwilling to accept the exposure implied by high haircuts.

6.1.2.4   Central Banks May Have Superior Information

A central bank may have, as bank supervisor, better information on the credit worthiness of banks in need of liquidity, compared with other market participants. Moreover, as a public entity not competing with banks, banks may be willing anyway to share private information with a central bank to establish their creditworthiness. In contrast, banks may be unwilling to reveal private information to competitors or private investors, even if this is made a pre-condition to obtaining funding from them. This may be particularly relevant when decisions need to be taken urgently.

6.1.2.5   LOLR as an Unconventional Monetary Policy at the ZLB

Taking LOLR measures may be decisive for a central bank to achieve its mandate to maintain price stability and to prevent the economy from falling into a deflationary trap. LOLR measures can prevent bank intermediation spreads from increasing in a crisis situation, which may be essential from a monetary policy perspective if the central bank has exhausted conventional monetary policy because of the zero lower bound (ZLB) on interest rates. This will be illustrated further by the model in Sect. 6.3.

6.2 Forms and Propensity to Act as LOLR

6.2.1 Forms of LOLR

The central bank LOLR function can take three forms: (a) LOLR built into the regular operational framework of the central bank; (b) LOLR added through changes of the framework and additional LOLR operations for all banks in crisis times; (c) emergency liquidity assistance to individual banks or, more rarely, even to non-banks. We consider these three one after the other.

LOLR built into the regular operational framework
The following elements determine the LOLR content of the regular operational framework.

- As mentioned earlier, **collateral availability** provides a first natural limit to central bank credit at the individual bank level. The volume of eligible collateral should also be viewed in relation to the liquidity deficit of the banking system to be covered by central bank credit operations. For example, in the case of the Eurosystem, the nominal value of eligible marketable assets has had a value of around EUR 14 trillion since 2012 (ECB 2020b), of which around EUR 5 trillion is held by banks, against a (pre-crisis, i.e. pre-2008) EUR 0.5 trillion liquidity deficit of the euro area banking system to be covered by credit operations. This implies that an average representative bank could extend, before hitting collateral constraints, recourse to central bank credit approximately 10 times relative to proportionality.
- The **ease at which central bank credit can be accessed**. In credit open market, the so-called "fixed-rate full allotment" procedure ensures that banks always get what they bid for. In a competitive auction, banks run a risk to not receive credit if they underestimate the aggressiveness with which other auction participants are bidding.
- Active **stigmatisation or de-stigmatisation** through central bank communication will impact on the propensity of banks to rely on the LOLR.
- It matters **who is able to access central bank credit and benefit directly from the LOLR**. Normally, only commercial banks have access to central bank credit, i.e. neither non-bank financials, nor non-financial corporates have.

Readiness of central banks to add LOLR content to the operational framework in crisis times
The impact of the LOLR on bank behaviour will not be limited to the LOLR content of the operational framework in normal times. What matters as well is the bank's liquidity in a scenario of financial market stress. Anticipating this case also includes building expectations on the readiness of the central bank to adjust the above-mentioned parameters that determine the LOLR content of the operational framework. Expectations will be determined by historical experience and forward-looking central bank communication.

Readiness of central banks to provide emergency liquidity assistance (ELA) to individual banks

ELA can be defined as a non-rule based LOLR activity for the benefit of individual banks. Of course, ELA also needs to take place within some legal framework, within the mandate of the central bank and ideally in a consistent manner. Limitations to ELA provision can result from:

(i) ELA collateral requirements (normally ELA collateral sets should be wider than the standard collateral set). (ii) Pricing of ELA, i.e. what surcharge relative to monetary policy credit operations is imposed (some surcharge is typically applied). (iii) Relevance to preserve systemic financial stability may be a precondition for granting ELA. The higher the hurdle set by the central bank in declaring a systemic financial stability interest before granting ELA, the less a bank can rely ex-ante on it, in particular if a bank is small. (iv) Limitations on the duration of ELA (ELA is typically assumed to be of limited duration). (v) Possible requirement that ELA is only granted if the central bank is protected in addition by a government guarantee. Beyond additional risk protection, this may be considered useful as it requires an elected government to confirm its backing of ELA operations (but it should not delay very urgent and obvious ELA provision by the central bank). (vi) ELA counterparty set: While normal central bank credit is only granted to banks, ELA could also be granted to any other financial corporate (or in theory even to any debtor).

6.2.2 Overall Propensity of a Central Bank to Act as LOLR

It is conceptually useful to first consider two extreme LOLR choices of the central bank.

- *Maximum LOLR*: accept in the normal-times operational framework all assets of banks as collateral at fair values without haircut. This would allow solvent banks to finance all their assets with the central bank, if desired, and no solvent counterparty could ever default for liquidity reasons. Furthermore, central bank credit is provided at a high frequency through fixed rate full allotment operations at the monetary policy target interest rate.
- *Minimum LOLR*: the central bank implements monetary policy only against risk-free assets, say AAA-rated Government paper. It largely covers its asset side through outright holdings of these AAA assets, and only conducts at the margin repos against the same assets. It conducts these small repos only with the highest rated counterparties. In this operational framework, banks have no discretionary access to central bank credit at all, i.e. the operational framework has no LOLR element. Moreover, the central bank would fully pre-commit to never change the LOLR content of its operational framework nor to ever provide ELA.

Central bankers believe that the optimal LOLR is in **between these two extremes**. The LOLR strengthens the ability of the financial system to provide maturity and liquidity transformation as services to society. At the same time, putting some limits to the LOLR role is beneficial for society, to have some protection against information asymmetries and moral hazard, to avoid relying excessively on the abilities of supervisors and auditors, and generally to preserve stronger incentives to maintain funding market access and thereby market discipline. Proponents of a tight approach may argue that a supportive LOLR will lead to as many financial crises as a very tight one, but crisis will be messier because when they occur the financial leverage will be much higher ("four-wheel vehicles make you get stuck in areas which are more difficult to access when you need to be rescued").

Assume for a moment that **we capture in the unit interval [0,1] the supportiveness of the LOLR framework** of a central bank and let the most restrictive framework described above be represented by 0 and the most forthcoming framework by 1 (it is of course a simplification to assume that designing the LOLR framework is a one-dimensional problem). One can map the LOLR unit interval into at least five effects, which should not be expected to be identical, although often this seems to be implicitly assumed:

(1) **Social welfare** is the ultimate measure of interest and can be equated, for example, with the extent to which the LOLR framework contributes to financial conditions leading to maximum economic growth in the medium to long term, i.e. through the financial and economic cycle. For example, Keister (2016) maps the LOLR supportiveness into social welfare, and Bindseil and Jablecki (2013) map it into growth. They show that it is likely that the relationship is a concave function with interior maximum (i.e. an intermediate LOLR maximizes growth).

(2) **Risk taking** is normally expected to increase monotonously for normal lenders when the readiness and ease of lending increases. For central banks, risk taking may be non-monotonous in the LOLR unit interval [0,1]. Bindseil and Jablecki (2013) provide an example in which the relationship is a convex function with interior minimum. As Bagehot's insight that sometimes "only the brave plan is the safe plan" suggests, the central bank cannot base its LOLR choices on the basis of the risk considerations that would apply for an "atomistic" investor not influencing the properties (e.g. default probabilities) of the system. Often, being more forthcoming as an LOLR after a negative financial stability shock (e.g. broadening the eligible collateral set to include less liquid assets) will decrease financial risk taking by the central bank, instead of increasing it. Risk endogeneity should lead to a more forthcoming LOLR, i.e. the welfare maximizing LOLR framework will be more supportive than the one obtained if risk endogeneity is ignored.

(3) **Leverage of banks** and their ability to provide liquidity and maturity transformation should increase monotonously with the supportiveness of the LOLR. Regulation may limit leverage to lower levels.

(4) **Financial fragility** will probably first decrease, and then increase across the LOLR unit interval, suggesting that a measured LOLR can stabilize the financial system while a too liberal one could eventually lead to particularly deep financial crises.

(5) **Market discipline and funding market functioning** can be thought of as
     either falling monotonously, or as mirroring the financial fragility curve, i.e.
     it would benefit from some moderate LOLR, but is undermined if the LOLR
     is excessive. Section 6.5 shows that when asset liquidity deteriorates after
     an exogenous shock, then the LOLR can preserve funding market access for
     solvent banks, but not for insolvent banks, while a restrictive LOLR will imply
     a run also on solvent banks. In this sense a more supportive LOLR can allow
     for a more effective market mechanism than a very restrictive one.

Moral hazard and central bank losses

A popular theme in papers on the LOLR is moral hazard, but the concept often
remains vague. One pragmatic view is that moral hazard only materializes in the
context of the LOLR if the central bank faces actual losses from its credit operations.
This interpretation also has the advantage that it would reduce the complexity of the
LOLR design problem by one dimension and map something vague and complex
(moral hazard) into something concrete and more measurable (central bank risk
taking—even if complicated by endogeneity). If central banks are worried about
moral hazard, they could tighten risk control measures (in normal times, to not be
pro-cyclical) so that the probability of central bank credit losses declines even further.

Excessive stigmatization of the LOLR?

Sometimes central banks worry that banks attach excessive stigma to recourse to the
LOLR. For example, recourse to the Discount Window is considered to remain stig-
matized in the US although the Fed has wanted to change this since 2002 (Armantier
et al. 2015). Also, in a number of credit open market operations of central banks
during the financial crisis, aversion of banks to participate materialized so that the
accommodation that the operations aimed at could not be achieved. Excessive stigma-
tization seems to go in the opposite direction of moral hazard. Central banks should
therefore have tools in hand to adjust *in both directions* the willingness of banks to
come to LOLR operations.

6.3 Central Bank Collateral as a Key LOLR Parameter in a Simple Bank Run Model

In this section we will integrate the LOLR in a bank-run model. In Sect. 6.3.1 we will
introduce a bank-run model in which a bank owns two kinds of assets, a completely
liquid asset and a completely illiquid asset. In Sect. 6.3.2, asset liquidity will be
described by means of a power function, which allows additional insights.

6.3.1 A Bank Run Model with Binary Levels of Asset Liquidity

Throughout this section, we consider the stylized bank balance sheet in **Table** 6.1. The total length of the balance sheet has been set to unity. Assets are grouped into two homogeneous classes in terms of asset liquidity and fire-sale discounts ($\Lambda \in [0,1]$). There are three types of liabilities, equity, long-term debt, and short-term deposits (with $e \in [0,1]$, $t \in [0,1]$ and $d \in [0,0.5]$).

The stylized balance sheet is sufficient to capture one key issue of banking: how to ensure the confidence of short-term depositors of the bank such that they do not easily withdraw deposits because of perceived credit risk, triggering self-fulfilling destructive dynamics ending in bank default. Confidence can be sustained by two means. *First*, the bank may limit the role of short-term funding. However, in general, households and institutional investors prefer to hold short-term debt instruments over long-term debt instruments and equity and request a higher return rate on the latter two types of claims, so that long-term debt and capital is associated with higher funding costs for the bank. *Second*, the bank may aim at holding sufficient amounts of liquid assets, both in the sense of being able to liquidate these assets in case of need, and to pledge them with the central bank at favourable haircuts. However, on average, liquid assets generate lower returns than illiquid ones. We now consider the representative bank in more detail.

6.3.1.1 Asset Liquidity and Central Bank Collateral Treatment

Assume two types of assets with extreme liquidity properties:

- A share Λ ($0 \leq \Lambda \leq 1$) of assets is **fully liquid** and can be sold without any fire-sale losses.
- A share $1 - \Lambda$ of assets is **totally illiquid**, i.e. if one tried to fire-sell these assets, one would not generate a cent of liquidity, but only losses.

At the same time, it is assumed that, when accepting bank assets as collateral, the central bank applies a homogeneous haircut h on all assets. In other words, the central bank haircut and collateral framework is not sensitive at all to asset liquidity.

Table 6.1 A stylised bank balance sheet to analyse funding stability of a bank

Bank			
Liquid assets	Λ	Short-term debt 1	d
Illiquid assets	$1 - \Lambda$	Short-term debt 2	d
		Long-term debt (term funding)	t
		Equity	e
Total assets	1	Total liabilities	1

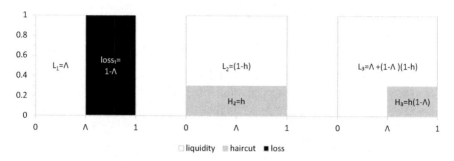

Fig. 6.1 Liquidity generation in a binary level of liquidity. Left: by liquidating all assets. Centre: by pledging all assets with the central bank. Right: liquidity-maximising combination

We summarise these assumptions in **Fig.** 6.1. Obviously in this case it never makes sense to fire-sell the illiquid assets as this would generate no liquidity but maximum losses. The illiquid assets should instead be pledged with the central bank. At the same time, to generate maximum liquidity, it makes sense to sell the liquid assets and to not pledge them.

6.3.1.2 Bank Liabilities

There are four types of liabilities: (i) *Short-term liabilities* are equally split to two ex-ante identical depositors; (ii) *Long-term debt* does not mature within the period considered and is ranked *pari passu* with short-term debt in case of liquidation of the bank; (iii) *Equity* is junior to all other liabilities and is also a stable funding source; (iv) *Central bank borrowing* is zero initially but can substitute for outflows of short-term liabilities in case of need.

6.3.1.3 Timeline

The model is based on the following timeline:

1. The asset parameters h and Λ are given
2. The bank chooses its liability composition, i.e. the parameters d and e.
3. Short-term depositors play a strategic game with two alternative actions: to run or not to run. "Running" means withdrawing deposits and transferring them to another account, accepting a small transaction cost ε.
4. It is not to be taken for granted that depositors can withdraw all their funds. If one or both of the depositors run, then at least one or several of the following will apply:

    (i) The bank substitutes lost deposit with central bank credit, assuming the bank has sufficient eligible collateral.

(ii)   Liquidation of assets: the bank may sell assets (but only when liquidation values exceed collateral values after haircuts).

(iii) If it is impossible to pay out the depositors that want to withdraw their deposits, illiquidity induced default occurs. After full liquidation took place, remaining depositors are paid out *pari passu*.

5.   If the bank was not closed due to illiquidity in the previous stage, its **solvency is assessed by the supervisor.** If capital is negative, the bank is liquidated and it is assumed in this case that the full costs of immediately liquidating all assets materialize. If it is still solvent, the bank survives.

6.3.1.4   Equilibrium

We use a *Strict Nash No-Run (SNNR)* equilibrium concept. The decision set of depositor i ($i = 1,2$) from which he will choose his decision D_i is $\{K_i, R_i\}$, where "K" stands for "keeping" deposits and "R" stands for "run". The payoff function of depositor i is: $U_i = U_i(D_1, D_2)$. The strategic game is symmetric, i.e. $U_1(K_1, K_2) = U_2(K_1, K_2)$, $U_1(K_1, R_2) = U_2(R_1, K_2)$, $U_1(R_1, K_2) = U_2(K_1, R_2)$, $U_1(R_1, R_2) = U_2(R_1, R_2)$. This allows us to express in the rest of the model conditions only with reference to one of the two players, say depositor 1.

A *Strict Nash equilibrium* is defined as a strategic game in which each player has a unique best response to the other players' strategies (see Fudenberg and Tirole 1991, 11). A *Strict Nash No-Run (SNNR) equilibrium* in the run game is therefore one in which the "no-run" choice dominates the "run" choice regardless of what the other depositors decide, i.e. an SNNR equilibrium is defined by:

$$U_1(K_1, K_2) > U_1(R_1, K_2) \cap U_1(K_1, R_2) > U_1(R_1, R_2)$$

A strict run equilibrium applies if $U_1(R_1, K_2) > U_1(K_1, K_2) \cap U_1(R_1, R_2) > U_1(K_1, R_2)$, and a multiple equilibrium case arises if $U_1(K_1, K_2) > U_1(R_1, K_2) \cap U_1(R_1, R_2) > U_1(K_1, R_2)$.

To identify the *cheapest sustainable funding structure*, we now define as a liquidity-stress strategy (LSS) of a bank a mapping of the assets of the bank into either their use as fire-sale reserves or as collateral for recourse to the central bank. In the chosen simple case, the choice of the LSS is trivial for the bank: liquid assets should be fire-sold, and illiquid assets should be pledged as collateral. This keeps liquidity generation capacity at a maximum and fire- sale losses at the minimum (zero). It is shown below that an SNNR applies if the liquidity generating power of the bank assets is at least equal to the deposits of one depositor, and equity is non-negative:

$$L = \Lambda + (1-\Lambda)(1-h) \geq d \quad \text{and} \quad e \geq 0$$

There are two possible states for solvency: either $e \geq 0$ (the bank is solvent), or $e < 0$ (the bank is insolvent). The liquidity condition can be divided into three cases: either liquidity is enough to pay out both depositors, or only one depositor, or neither. **Table** 6.2 shows the depositor's equilibrium decision for the resulting six cases (because of symmetry it is the same for both players).

If equity is negative, run is always the equilibrium choice. If equity is positive a no-run equilibrium can be ensured if liquidity is sufficient to pay out one depositor. In establishing the payoffs in case of liquidation, we take a simplifying assumption, namely that the central bank, liquidating the assets pledged by the bank after default, recovers exactly the liquidity it had provided through the pledge, while the security buffer granted by the haircut is completely depleted, i.e. equal to $L = \Lambda + (1 - \Lambda)(1 - h)$. Under this assumption payoffs can be calculated in scenarios of liquidity-induced defaults by just taking the pay-outs before the moment of default.

6.3.1.5   Positive Equity

First, we analyse cases (1) to (3), in which equity is positive.

(1)   **Table** 6.3 shows the precise pay-offs if there is enough liquidity to pay out both depositors, keeping is a superior strategy whatever the other depositor does, as it allows us to save ε, the cost of running (Table 6.3).

(2)   If liquidity is sufficient for paying out only one depositor, i.e. $d \leq L < 2d$, the bank run game takes the payoffs as shown in **Table** 6.4.

That (K_1, K_2) is the unique solution for both cases can be shown by directly applying the definition of the SNNR equilibrium. In the second case, in the hypothetical case that both depositors ran (which they should not), the bank balance sheet would look as **in Table** 6.5 at the moment of default. The bank will have fire-sold all its liquid assets, and pledged all its non-liquid assets. The assumption that the central bank will "consume" the haircut when liquidating the asset implies that the losses in collateral liquidation will exceed and consume the previous equity of the bank.

Table 6.2 Equilibrium decision of depositors depending on liquidity and solvency of the bank

		Solvency condition	
		$e \geq 0$	$e < 0$
Liquidity condition	$L \geq 2d$	(1) keep	(4) run
	$d \leq L \leq 2d$	(2) keep	(5) run
	$L < d$	(3) keep/run	(6) run

Table 6.3 Pay-offs to depositors if $L \geq 2d$ and $e \geq 0$

$\downarrow D_1, D_2 \rightarrow$	K_2	R_2
K_1	**d, d**	d, d $- \varepsilon$
R_1	d $- \varepsilon$, d	d $- \varepsilon$, d $- \varepsilon$

Table 6.4 Pay-offs to depositors if $d \leq L < 2d$ and $e \geq 0$

D_1, D_2	K_2	R_2
K_1	**d, d**	$d, d - \varepsilon$
R_1	$d - \varepsilon, d$	$L/2 - \varepsilon, L/2 - \varepsilon,$

Table 6.5 Bank's balance sheet at the moment of default in the non-equilibrium run scenario $L = \Lambda + (1 - \Lambda)(1 - h)$

Bank			
Liquid assets (sold)	0	Short-term debt 1	$d - L/2$
Illiquid assets (pledged)	$1 - \Lambda$	Short-term debt 2	$d - L/2$
		Long-term debt	$1 - e - 2d$
		Equity	e
		Central-bank funding	$(1 - h)(1 - \Lambda)$
Total assets	$(1 - \Lambda)$	Total liabilities	$(1 - \Lambda)$

Table 6.6 Pay-offs to depositors if $L < d$ and $e \geq 0$

D_1, D_2	K_2	R_2
K_1	**d, d**	$0, L - \varepsilon$
R_1	$L - \varepsilon, 0$	**$L/2 - \varepsilon, L/2 - \varepsilon$**

All deposits that could not be withdrawn, as well as all long-term claims and equity are lost because following our assumption regarding collateral liquidation by the central bank, the liquidation of the pledged assets will suffice to just repay central-bank funding.

(3)   **Table** 6.6 shows pay-offs if liquidity is insufficient to pay out even one depositor, but equity is still non-negative. Two equilibriums emerge: one in with both depositors stay with their deposits, and one, inferior, in which they both run, causing default and the related losses.

Running is now an equilibrium because if the other depositor runs, and you don't, then you end up with zero value as the liquidation of the bank will lead to a zero recovery ratio. In contrast, if you are the one who runs and the other doesn't, then you recover $L > 0$, while if you also do not run, you recover only $L/2$.

6.3.1.6   Negative Equity

If equity is negative, the bank will eventually be closed and its assets will be liquidated by the regulator. By definition, the recover ratio r with negative equity will be $0 < r < 1$ of their claims, while $1 - r$ will be the loss-given default. Depositors can try to withdraw their deposits without losses before liquidation and the more a depositor

withdraws, the more the losses will be dumped on the other creditors who will have
a higher loss-given-default. As the game is symmetric, there will be a unique run
equilibrium. We call $r = 1 + e$ (with $e < 0$) the recovery ratio in the absence of runs,
i.e. the recovery ratio that would be equally applied to short-term and long-term
creditors in this case. We call r' the recovery ratio for the remaining creditors if only
one depositor runs, and r" the one if both depositors run. Clearly, $0 \le r" \le r' \le r \le 1$.

(4)   **Table** 6.7 shows pay-off if liquidity is enough to pay out both depositors:

- If no depositor runs, both depositors will recover a share r of their deposit
  after liquidation.
- If one depositor runs, one will completely recover her deposit and the other
  deposit a share r' after liquidation.
- If both run (equilibrium solution), both will recover all their deposits, all
  losses will fall on the long-term creditor.

(5)   **Table** 6.8 shows pay-offs if liquidity is enough to pay only one depositor:

- If none run: they will recover a share r of their deposit after liquidation,
  which is exactly the same as in case 4
- If only one runs: she will recover her full deposit, while the other depositor
  will recover a share r' after liquidation
- If both run: there is not enough liquidity to withdraw all deposits. They will
  withdraw an amount equal to the whole disposable liquidity and divide them
  proportionally on each's share of the total deposit. The long-term creditor
  will lose all his capital, as we assumed that the sale of the bank's asset will
  not provide any further amount beyond what is provided by the central bank

(6)   Finally, **Table** 6.9 shows the pay-offs if liquidity is not enough even for paying
out a single depositor, the depositor that runs will be able to recover at least
part of its credit without haircut, both r' and r" are equal to zero.

Table 6.7 Pay-offs to depositors if $L \ge 2d$ and $e < 0$

D_1, D_2	K_2	R_2
K_1	r d, r d	r' d - ε, d - ε
R_1	d − ε, r' d − ε	**d − ε, d − ε**

Table 6.8 Pay-offs to depositors if $d \le L < 2d$ and $e < 0$

D_1, D_2	K_2	R_2
K_1	rd, rd	r'd, d − ε
R_1	d − ε, r'd	**L/2 − ε, L/2 − ε**

Table 6.9 Pay-offs to depositors if L < d and e < 0

D_1, D_2	K_2	R_2
K_1	rd, rd	$0, L - \varepsilon$
R_1	$L - \varepsilon, 0$	$L/2 - \varepsilon, L/2 - \varepsilon$

Table 6.10 Utility of depositor 1 depending on own and depositor 2's decisions: $U_1(D_1D_1)$

		(1)	(2)	(3)	(4)	(5)	(6)
		$e \geq 0$			$e < 0$		
D_1	D_2	$L \geq 2d$	$2d > L \geq d$	$L < d$	$L \geq 2d$	$2d > L \geq d$	$L < d$
K_1	K_2	d	d	d	Rd	rd	rd
K_1	R_2	d	d	0	r'd	r'd	r'd=0
R_1	K_2	$d - \varepsilon$	$d - \varepsilon$	$L - \varepsilon$	$d - \varepsilon$	$d - \varepsilon$	$L - \varepsilon$
R_1	R_2	$d - \varepsilon$	$L/2 - \varepsilon$	$L/2 - \varepsilon$	$d - \varepsilon$	$L/2 - \varepsilon$	$L/2 - \varepsilon$

In **Table** 6.10 we summarise the results showing the payoffs for player 1. The shaded area indicates where the bank is liquidated. The areas with bold larger font are the equilibrium solutions of the run game.

6.3.1.7   Central Bank Collateral Easing to Restore Financial Stability in a Financial Crisis

Asset liquidity (as captured by the parameter Λ) **and asset values can change over time, and also the central bank may change haircuts over time**. For example, **Fig.** 6.3 (from Dötz and Weth 2019, 12) illustrates how asset liquidity fluctuates over time. Moreover, asset values can change, which is reflected in a change of equity. For example, if initial equity is 0.2 and total assets 1, then a decline of asset values by more than 20% depletes equity and therefore pushes the bank into a single run equilibrium. Asset value deterioration also leads to a deterioration of the liquidity condition, as it leads to a shrinkage of liquidity relative to short term debt.

To what extent **can the collateral framework of the central bank as captured by h make a difference for funding stability?** First, obviously h does not impact on solvency. Therefore, whenever e < 0 we are unavoidably in the case of the single bank run equilibrium. Central banks should not combat financial instability due to negative equity with collateral policies. However, h can make the difference for meeting the liquidity condition. We can calculate the maximum haircut compatible with a single no-run equilibrium from the condition of sufficient liquidity. Therefore, it is easy to show that decreases of h can compensate both unexpected asset value declines and a drop of the share of liquid assets in terms of restoring the condition $L > d$, assuming that equity remained positive.

Cheapest stable funding structure
If the bank does not fear a deterioration of asset values or a decline of the share of liquid assets, it will choose **the cheapest liability structure that is just supporting a single no-run equilibrium**. If cost of equity is higher than the cost of long-term debt, the bank will, in the model above, however not issue any equity and achieve its competitive stable funding structure only through sufficient long-term funding. This is the limitation of the simplest model setting: it does not allow modelling equity as a safeguard against fire-sale losses, and therefore does not contribute to a better understanding of the full liability structure including equity. Consider the following example: if $\Lambda = 0.3$ and $h = 0.8$ then the funding structure maximising short term deposits is the one in which $d = 0.44$, i.e. $t + e = 0.12$ and $e \geq 0$. For any (i_t, i_e) with $i_t < i_e$, the cheapest stable funding structure will be $e = 0$, $d = 0.88$, and $t = 0.12$.

6.3.1.8 Collateral Policies as Monetary Policies at the ZLB

Broadening the collateral set in a liquidity crisis may be a key monetary policy measure, in particular when conventional monetary policy has hit the zero lower bound. The simple bank- run model above allowed us to show that when asset liquidity deteriorates, then banks need to move to a more expensive bank liability structure. If they do so quickly enough, the bank-run equilibrium may not materialize. But a more expensive capital structure means that the spread between the short-term risk-free interest rate (controlled by the central bank) and the actual bank financing costs, and thus bank lending rates, increase. The central bank could maintain financial conditions unchanged by lowering the short-term risk-free interest rate. This is however not an option if the zero lower bound has been reached. The central bank **could therefore broaden its collateral framework so as to make the old, cheap bank liability structure stable again**.

We illustrate the last point further with the bank balance sheet in Table 6.11.

This bank has stable short term funding if $L = \Lambda + (1 - \Lambda)(1 - h) \geq d/2 \Rightarrow d^* = 1 - h + h\Lambda$, with d obviously capped at 1. Assume that the financial conditions ("FC") are equal to bank lending rates, and these are equal to the average funding costs of the

Table 6.11 Effectiveness of collateral policies at the zero lower bound

Bank			
Liquid assets	Λ	Short term debt 1	d/2
Illiquid assets	$1 - \Lambda$	Short term debt 2	d/2
		Long term debt	$1 - d$
Total assets	1	Total liabilities	1

banks, as banks would be perfectly efficient, i.e. would not have any administrative costs and be within a competitive sector. Also assume that the funding costs of short-term deposits is equal to i, the risk-free short-term interest rate, which is the monetary policy interest rate set by the central bank. Assume that the cost of long-term funding is equal to the sum of the short-term risk-free lending rate, i, plus the term premium, ω. Therefore: $FC = id + (i + \omega)(1 - d) = i + \omega - \omega d$.

By substituting the highest possible share of short-term deposits which ensures stable funding, we obtain[1]: $FC = i + \omega - \omega 2(1 - h + h\Lambda) \Leftrightarrow FC = i + \omega (2 h(1 - \Lambda) - 1)$. In words: financial conditions tighten (funding costs increase) with (i) short-term risk-free interest rates, (ii) the equity risk premium, (iii) the haircuts imposed by the central bank, (iv) the share of illiquid assets. Therefore, when the zero lower bound is reached for conventional monetary policy, then haircuts can contribute to achieve the adequate monetary policy (i.e. the adequate financial conditions), and **a decrease in haircuts can be a measure necessary to compensate for an increase of the equity risk premium or a deterioration of asset liquidity**. Of course, such a lowering of haircuts for monetary policy purposes should not imply that the role of haircuts to protect the central bank from losses should be forgotten, i.e. the central bank will face a trade-off between monetary policy objectives and risk objectives.

6.3.2 The Model with Continuous Asset Liquidity

In this model variant (Bindseil 2013), one assumes that (i) **assets are continuous in terms of liquidity properties**, that (ii) they are equally ranked from both the fire-sale loss and central bank haircut perspectives, and that (iii) both haircuts and fire-sale discounts have the functional form across the assets of a power function, i.e. haircuts are $h(x) = x^\delta$ and marginal fire sale losses are $f(x) = x^\theta$ with $\delta > 0$ and $\theta > 0$, i.e. θ summarises the liquidation cost function and δ the central bank haircut function. This continuous approach to asset liquidity and central bank haircuts has a number of advantages: (i) it allows us to differentiate between the roles of equity and long-term debt; (ii) it is more realistic than the assumptions taken on assets so far; (iii) the power function is tractable in the context of our model.

Consider first the case when the central bank does not at all act as lender of last resort, i.e. the only source of liquidity generation in the case of a run is to fire-sell assets. If a certain share x of the bank's assets has to be sold, then the fire-sale discounts will have to be booked as a loss and reduce equity. Assuming that the bank starts with the most liquid assets and sells a share x of total asset, the total fire sale loss will be:

$$F(x, \theta) = \int_{s=0}^{x} s^\theta ds = \frac{x^{\theta+1}}{\theta + 1}$$

[1]Note that the multiplier of ω will be positive for the assumption that $2d^* < 1$. Indeed $2d^* = 2(1 - h + h\Lambda) < 1 \Rightarrow -2 h(1 - \Lambda) < -1 \Rightarrow h(1 - \Lambda) > 1/2$.

As mentioned in Chap. 5, empirical estimates of default costs in the corporate finance literature vary between 10% and 44%. This cost can be interpreted as the liquidation cost of assets, captured in the parameter θ. Liquidation of all assets will lead to a damage of $F(1) = 1/(1 + \theta)$, and sales proceeds (cash generated) will be $1 - F(1) = \theta/(1 + \theta)$. Consequently, θ can be calculated as $\theta = (1 - F(1))/F(1)$. If default cost is 10%, this would mean that $\theta = 9$, and if default cost is 44%, then $\theta = 1.27$. For a value of default costs in the middle of the empirical estimates of say 25%, one obtains $\theta = 3$.

In **Fig.** 6.2 below, we illustrate this approach by showing the distribution between liquidity generation and asset fire-sale losses under the assumption of a power function of fire-sale costs and ranked asset from the most to the least liquid, **for the range of the empirical estimates of costs of default**, i.e. for 10% (implying $\theta = 9$) and 44% (implying $\theta = 1.25$). Moreover, we show the power function to replicate the estimated recovery ratio in the case of the Lehman Brothers of 28%, i.e. default costs of 72% under the assumption that before default, Lehman had zero equity (Fleming and Sarkar 2014a, b).

That asset liquidity is continuous, and that it fluctuates over time, has been described empirically in the finance literature, such as recently in Dötz and Weth (2019), who also argue that liquidation will be carried out in a liquidity pecking order style and that marginal liquidation costs should be expected to increase in redemptions. They construct a sample of corporate bond fund asset liquidity data covering the 80 months before June 2016, referring to around 700 thousand security holdings positions. Price and liquidity information are added to each such position. The liquidity measure consists in monthly averages derived from daily bid-ask spreads. **Figure** 6.3 shows continuous portfolio liquidity, put at any moment in time into a "liquidity pecking order" (i.e. securities ranked from the most to the least liquid). Obviously, the least liquid assets held by a corporate bond fund will still be more liquid than many other bank assets (e.g. loan portfolios). Still, it nicely illustrates the idea of continuous asset liquidity and the changes of asset liquidity over time.

Assume that in the case of a bank run, the bank does whatever it takes in terms of asset liquidation to avoid **illiquidity induced default**. The total amount of liquidity that the bank can generate through asset fire sales is $\theta/(\theta + 1)$. Therefore, illiquidity

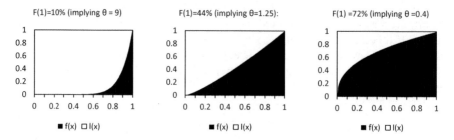

Fig. 6.2 Three representations of fire sale losses and liquidity generation assuming that marginal fire sale losses f(x) are a power function with exponent theta

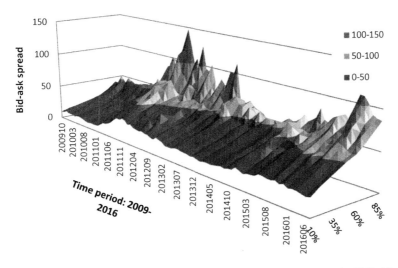

Fig. 6.3 Liquidity structure of corporate bond funds, according to Dötz and Weth (2019, 12)

induced default will materialise only if deposit withdrawals eventually exceed this amount. Two default triggering events need to be considered. Indeed, even if the bank has survived a liquidity withdrawal, it may afterwards be assessed as insolvent and thus be liquidated at the request of the bank supervisor. As noted above, for a given liquidity withdrawal x, the fire-sale related loss is $x^{\theta+1}/(\theta + 1)$ (Fig. 6.3).

Default due to insolvency occurs if this loss exceeds initial equity, i.e. $e < x^{\theta + 1}/(\theta + 1)$.[2] It can be shown (see e.g. Bindseil 2013, proposition 2) that a single no-run equilibrium exists if and only if (and assuming again the bank liability structure shown at the beginning of Sect. 6.5) both a liquidity and a solvency condition are fulfilled:

$$\theta/(\theta + 1) \geq d \quad \text{and} \quad e \geq d^{\theta+1}/(\theta + 1).$$

The liquidity condition is similar to the discrete case: to ensure financial stability in the case of absence of central bank credit, the liquidity generating capacity of the bank needs to correspond at least to the deposits of one of the two depositors. The solvency condition expresses an aspect that could not be captured in the discrete case: the financial damage suffered by generating through fire sales the liquidity needed to pay out one of the two depositors must not exceed the bank's equity.

What is the **cheapest sustainable liability structure** in this model? For given θ, competing banks will always go to the limit in terms of the cheapest possible liability structure as determined by the conditions in the strategic depositor game, such that the no-run equilibrium is still maintained as an SNNR equilibrium. Assume that the

---

[2]Note that it is assumed that equity is never sufficient to absorb the losses resulting from a bank default, i.e. it is assumed that $e \leq 1/(\theta + 1)$. Of course, one could also calculate through the opposite case, but it is omitted here as it does not seem to match reality.

cost of remuneration of the three asset types are r_e for equity, r_t for term funding, and 0 for short term deposits. Also assume that $r_e > r_t > 0$. In this setting what will the composition of the banks' liabilities be? The objective of choosing a liability composition will be to minimize the average overall remuneration rate subject to maintaining a stable short-term funding basis. The two minimum conditions to be fulfilled are $\theta/(1 + \theta) = d$ and $e = d^{(1+\theta)}/(1 + \theta)$. These conditions can be solved for a unique optimum e^*, d^*, and hence also for the average necessary remuneration rate of bank liabilities t^* being $r_t + e^* r_e$.

If the central bank offers collateralised credit
Now consider **the case in which also the pledging of collateral with the central bank is possible**. To obtain outcomes in which the banks rely both on fire sales and haircuts in their liquidity stress strategy, we obviously need $\delta > \theta$ (otherwise it is always superior to only pledge and never to fire-sale). It can be shown in the non-trivial case that the bank's liquidity stress strategy will always foresee the share z of most liquid assets to be fire-sold, while the rest, the $1 - z$ less liquid assets, will be pledged with the central bank. The condition for an SNNR is provided in proposition 5 of Bindseil (2013):

Let z in [0,1] determine which share of its assets is foreseen by the bank to be used for fire sales (i.e. the less liquid share $1 - z$ of assets are foreseen for pledging with the central bank). Let $F = F(z)$ be the fire-sale losses from fire selling the z most liquid assets and let $L = L(z)$ be the total liquidity generated from fire-selling the most liquid assets z and from pledging the least liquid assets $(1 - z)$. Then a single no run equilibrium exists if and only if

$$\exists z \in [0, 1] : L = L(z) = \frac{\delta}{\delta + 1} + \frac{z^{\delta+1}}{\delta + 1} - \frac{z^{(\theta+1)}}{\theta + 1} \geq d$$

.

and

$$F = F(z) = \frac{z^{(\theta+1)}}{\theta + 1} \leq e$$

In contrast to the discrete model variant, this variant allows us to explain the full capital structure, including the distinction between long-term debt and equity, and the roles of these two funding sources can be shown to depend on the relative cost of the two and the relative size of δ compared to θ.

The model and its solution are illustrated in **Fig. 6.4**. The vertical line z separates the liquidity-ranked asset space into the part that will be fire-sold (assets on the left of z, i.e. most liquid assets) and the part that will be pledged (assets on the right of z, i.e. least liquid assets). The bank foresees in its liquidity stress strategy to fire-sale the assets [0,z] and to incur fire-sale losses of F, and generate liquidity through fire sales equal to L_1. Moreover, in this strategy the bank pledges the assets [z,1] and generates through this liquidity equal to L_2. Therefore, total liquidity generated (which must

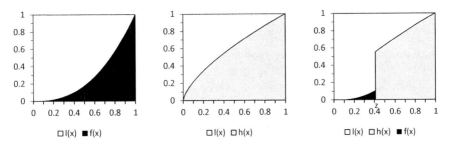

Fig. 6.4 Liquidity generation and fire sales in a model of continuous asset liquidity. Left: using fire sales, centre: using pledging at the Central Bank, right: using box

Table 6.12 Bank financed only by short term debt and equity

Bank A			
Assets	1	Depositor 1	d
		Depositor 2	d
		Equity	1 − 2d
Total	1	Total	1

at least be equal to the deposits of one depositor) is $L_1 + L_2$ and total fire-sale losses are F (which must not exceed equity e).

To calculate the relevant surfaces as illustrated in Fig. 6.4, we only need to apply that the integral of x^a in $[0,z]$ is equal to $z^{(a+1)}/(a+1)$. L_1 is the surface above the fire-sale loss function up to z (the liquidity generated from fire sales); F is the surface below the fire-sale loss function up to z (the losses generated from the sales), and L_2 is the surface above the haircut function between z and 1 (the liquidity generated by pledging assets).

$$L_1 = z - B = z - \frac{z^{\theta+1}}{\theta + 1} \qquad F = \frac{z^{\theta+1}}{\theta + 1} \qquad L_2 = 1 - \frac{1}{\delta + 1} - \left(z - \frac{z^{\delta+1}}{\delta + 1}\right)$$

Example: assume that banks' liabilities consist only of equity and short-term debt, such as in Table 6.12.

Also assume that initially $\theta = 1.4$, $\delta = 0.5$ and $e = 0.2$ so that each depositor has deposits of 0.4. One can now calculate that with $z = 0.5$, one obtains liquidity generating power $L = 0.49$ and associated fire-sale losses $F = 0.08$ (this is easily done by putting the formulas of the surfaces L_1, F, L_2 from the chart above into Excel). This allows for a single no-run funding equilibrium.

6.4   Conclusions

The following five key conclusions can be drawn from the simple bank run model (and taking various simplifying model assumption as described, including that banks and depositors have the same perfect information on asset values, asset liquidity, and bank liability composition): First, both asset value and asset liquidity deterioration can trigger a run. Second, insufficient liquidity leads to multiple equilibria, while negative equity always implies a run. Therefore, the LOLR (i.e. captured in this simple setting by central bank collateral haircuts) will never stop a run if equity is negative. However, LOLR action can restore a single no-run equilibrium when only an asset liquidity deterioration and/or an asset value deterioration occurs, as long as equity remains positive. Third, tightening collateral rules can destabilize banks by pushing them into the multiple equilibrium case. Fourth, if an asset liquidity deterioration pushes banks into the multiple equilibrium case without the run equilibrium materializing, banks will be incentivized to adjust their capital structure so as to restore the single no-run equilibrium case. This typically leads to a more expensive capital structure, i.e. to more expensive bank intermediation and hence, everything else equal, a tightening of monetary and financial conditions. If monetary policy has reached the zero lower bound, increasing collateral availability can be an effective monetary policy tool. Fifth, if banks through competition and myopic behaviour tend to converge to the cheapest sustainable liability structure, then very small shocks on asset value and asset liquidity can destroy funding stability. It may therefore be useful to impose liquidity regulation on banks.

Chapter 7
International Monetary Frameworks

In this chapter we turn to representing flows of funds in alternative international monetary frameworks, and what global liquidity these different frameworks provide. We first recall some arguments in favour of and against fixed exchange rate systems. We then introduce two international monetary arrangements of the past which imply fixed exchange rates, namely the gold standard and the Bretton Woods system, and recall why both eventually failed. We then turn to three international monetary frameworks in the context of the current paper standard, i.e. fixed exchange rate systems, flexible exchange rate systems, and the European monetary union. We explain the role of an international lender of last resort and related solutions, and how these allow for more leeway in running fixed exchange rate systems. We also show how banks and central bank balance sheets are affected by international flows of funds and the balance of payments. Finally, we briefly review recent developments of foreign currency reserves, being the key central bank balance sheet position in this context.

7.1 Why Do Fixed Exchange Rates Persist?

This chapter introduces the flow of funds mechanics of various international monetary frameworks. It will be shown how the frameworks absorb capital and current account imbalances and see what limits the systems may encounter. Most of the sections of this chapter are devoted to forms of fixed exchange rate systems. International monetary frameworks often aimed at supporting fixed exchange rate systems, or they imply by construction fixed rates, like the international gold standard. Under fixed exchange rates, the central bank loses its otherwise unconstrained LOLR powers in its domestic currency. In addition, with fixed exchange rates, central banks lose the power to do independent monetary policy, as monetary policy will be determined by the need to be consistent with the fixed exchange rate. Obstfeld and Rogoff (1995) have therefore concluded that "for most countries, it is folly to recapture the lost innocence of fixed

© The Author(s) 2021
U. Bindseil and A. Fotia, *Introduction to Central Banking*,
SpringerBriefs in Quantitative Finance,
https://doi.org/10.1007/978-3-030-70884-9_7

exchange rates". Why do countries or central banks want to have fixed exchange rates at all, or bind themselves to gold so as to lose parts of their freedom and power, both in terms of monetary policy, and as a lender-of-last resort? For example, why has the EU launched the euro project and why has China shown so much commitment over the last decades to keep its exchange rates relatively stable by allowing its foreign reserves to fluctuate considerably?

Mainly four reasons for fixed exchange rates are still sometimes considered valid:

- Effective fixed exchange rates make it possible to achieve **the network benefits from a more universal money**. Exchange rate stability contributes to reduce uncertainty and transaction costs (as currency dealers do not need to be compensated for risk taking or for being occasionally exploited by insiders). In particular, for a small country, it can be welfare improving to give up its own monetary freedom and to link its currencies to make its own economy benefit from a larger de facto monetary area.
- Binding a currency to gold or to another stable currency may make it possible to obtain credibility as it provides a commitment that can be monitored and that anchors expectations. A commitment to a certain inflation rate is not observable on a day-by-day basis as inflation is linked to policy measures only in a noisy and lagged way. The success of binding a currency to another one (or to gold) can be monitored on a continuous basis.
- Establish an order to **prevent "beggar my neighbour" foreign exchange policies or "exchange rate wars"**. For some episodes, observers have felt that exchange rate policies in flexible exchange rate systems have been used to achieve devaluations of their own currencies to make domestic industries more competitive and thereby stimulate domestic growth—at the expense of trading partners who experience exactly opposite effects in a sort of zero-sum game. A fixed exchange rate system, in particular with some agreed rules and a governance framework, could be seen as a way to overcome incentives for such non-cooperative behaviour which at the end makes everybody worse off.
- **Variable exchange rate systems may have a tendency to "overshoot"**, i.e. volatility of exchange rates is not just reflecting changing real factors, but additional, endogenously created volatility, not only related to speculation and panics, but also with sticky prices, as Dornbush (1976) noticed a few years after the breakdown of the Bretton Woods System.

For these reasons, countries have often chosen to try to fix their currency to a precious metal or to other currencies. Different forms of fixed currencies systems exist, as will be explained below (e.g. peg to metal; unilateral peg to another currency; multilateral agreement like the Bretton woods framework; EMS; monetary union). In the following sections, four international monetary arrangements will be introduced. First, frameworks of the past: the gold standard, which had its height from around 1875 to 1914, and second the Bretton Woods System, which regulated the international monetary relation from 1945 to 1971 and was officially dissolved in 1976.

Then, arrangements that are still in place today: fixed exchange rates and flexible exchange rates in the context of a paper standard.

7.2 Past International Monetary Frameworks

7.2.1 The Gold Standard

To represent the flow of funds under an international gold standard, assume two countries $i = \{1,2\}$, and the following for each sector:

- **Households** are not leveraged, they initially held all real assets of the economy, including gold, but they were ready to give up a part of it, "G_i", and hold instead extra deposits with their home bank. Therefore, their initial deposits with their home bank are $D_i + G_i$. Households hold banknotes equal to B in their domestic currency.
- **Corporates** are identical across the two countries and financed exclusively through bank loans. They hold the real assets given up by the household (with the exception of gold).
- The two **banking systems** are also identical initially. Each banking system has assets of $D_i + B_i$ and is financed through bank deposits $(D_i + G_i)$ and through central bank credit $(B_i - G_i)$.
- Each of the **central banks** has a balance sheet length of B_i, equal to banknotes issued. In terms of assets, this is matched partially by the gold holdings (G_i) and partially credited to banks $(B_i - G_i)$.

Cross border economic flows (financial flows and those relating to trade) are captured in the balance of payment, which records the economic transactions of a country within the international context. For a detailed description of the international accounting standards of the balance of payment, see the IMF Balance of Payments Manual (IMF 2009). Here, the flow of funds analysis will be limited to basic trade and financial flow transactions. For example, the following two events, which also affect the international accounts of a country, will not be captured:

- *Changes of asset valuation.* Changes of values of cross border asset and liability positions affects the international accounts of a country. In a flexible exchange rate system, many such valuation changes stem from exchange rate adjustments, but they will not be limited to them: for example, a cross border claim in the form of equity fluctuates in value even if exchange rates do not change. The net foreign wealth position of a country will be affected as well.
- *Transfers, remittances, indemnities.* Transactions of this type are international transfers through donations (e.g. a rich country provides development aid to a poor country by giving real goods or money), remittances (a Pakistani accountant working in Abu Dhabi transfers money every month to his family in Pakistan); a

country winning a war imposes an indemnity to the country that lost it; a country grants debt relief to another.

Table 7.1 shows basic capital and current account transactions defined as follows.

Capital transactions (ca): We define a capital transaction as one in which net financial claims between sectors of countries change without transfer of real goods (other than gold). In the gold standard, they are settled in central bank gold. We assume that household 2 is behind the capital move, namely that household 2 opens an account with bank 1 and then shifts a part of her bank deposit from country 2 into country 1. There are different ways of imagining how these transfers can concretely take place. Capital account transactions do not change the net foreign position of a country, i.e. having a net credit or a net debt towards the rest of the world. But in a fixed exchange rate system, they typically change the net cross-border position of the private sector, with opposite changes of the public sector as represented by the central bank.

Current account transactions (cu): Here we assume that household 1 sells a real asset to household B (alternatively, the transaction could also take place between corporates). Household 2 instructs her bank to credit the account of household 1 with bank 1. Again, this transaction can be implemented in different ways. At the end, it will impact on accounts as shown in Table 7.1. Current account transactions normally change the **net foreign position** of a country, i.e. the difference between foreign assets and foreign liabilities of a country.

Table 7.2 shows these accounts in the form of an asset liability matrix (see Table 7.2), such as introduced in Sect. 2.2.1.

If for example $ca = -cu$, then under fixed exchange rates (including the gold standard), the central bank gold (or foreign exchange) reserves do not change. This means that in net terms, capital flows exactly finance the net transfer of goods. There are single transactions that represent both types of transactions at once, for example: a machine is exported from corporate 1 to corporate 2, but not paid yet, such that a financial claim from corporate 1 to corporate 2 is created at the same time when the real good passes the border. This transaction takes place entirely in the corporate sector balance sheets. In the accounts below (Table 7.3), the value of the transaction is denoted by X, with $\mathbf{X = cu = -ca}$.

Capital and current account balances can have various reasons:

- **Smoothing the consumption path of households**: for example, one country may have a particularly low birth rate, and its households could partially invest their savings abroad, allowing it to transfer consumption into the future.
- Growth rates, and hence **real rates of return, may be higher in one country than in another**. Therefore, the rates of return on capital investments should also be higher in that country. Real assets are likely to move into this country for production purposes, and the flow of real goods could be financed by capital inflows. In this case (and similarly in the previous one), the balance of payment may be balanced as capital and current accounts tend to compensate each other. But the net foreign position of the country would change, as the country would become indebted towards the rest of the world.

Table 7.1 Two countries' financial accounts, gold standard

Household 1			
Deposits Bank 1	$D_1 + G_1 + cu$	Household Equity	E_1
Banknotes	B_1		
Real Assets	$E_1 - D_1 - B_1 - G_1 - cu$		
Corporate 1			
Real assets	$D_1 + B_1$	Loans Bank 1	$D_1 + B_1$
Bank 1			
Loans corporate 1	$D_1 + B_1$	Deposits household 1	$D_1 + G_1 + cu$
		Deposits household 2	$+ ca$
		Credit central bank 1	$B_1 - G_1 - ca - cu$
Central Bank 1			
Credit Bank	$B_1 - G_1 - ca - cu$	Banknotes issued	B_1
Gold reserves	$G + ca + cu$		
Household 2			
Deposits Bank 2	$D_2 + G_2 - ca - cu$	Household Equity	E_2
Deposits Bank 1	$+ ca$		
Banknotes 2	B_2		
Real Assets	$E_2 - D_2 - B_2 - G_2 + cu$		
Corporate 2			
Real assets	$D_2 + B_2$	Loans Bank 2	$D_2 + B_2$
Bank 2			
Loans corporate 2	$D_2 + B_2$	Deposits household 2	$D_2 + G_2 - ca - cu$
		Credit central bank 2	$B_2 - G_2 + ca + cu$
Central Bank 2			
Credit Bank	$B_2 - G_2 + ca + cu$	Banknotes issued	B_2
Gold reserves	$G_2 - ca - cu$		

- There is also the case where **capital and current account imbalances both have the same sign and therefore contribute jointly to a payment imbalance**. For example, although not under a gold standard, emerging market economies like China in the first decade of 2000 had both large capital inflows and large current account surpluses. Capital goods were imported to China, but exports in consumer goods were so strong that the current account was in surplus. Foreign reserves ballooned in China during this period (under the gold standard its gold reserves would have ballooned). Greece in 2010 seems to have represented the opposite case, i.e. it had both a capital account and a current account deficit.
- **Capital accounts can be driven by capital flight and then the amplitude of the capital account easily exceeds that of the current account**. This was illustrated

Table 7.2 Two countries' financial accounts, gold standard, matrix representation

Asset of: →	Real assets ↓	Liability of: ↓								Tot Financial Assets	Tot Assets
		HH A	HH B	Corp 1	Corp 2	Bank 1	Bank 2	CB 1	CB 2		
Real Equity→	$E_1 + E_2$	E	E								
Household 1	$(E_1 - D_1 - B_1) - G_1 - cu$					$D_1 + G_1 + cu$		B_1		$D_1 + B_1 + G_1 + cu$	E_1
Household 2	$(E_2 - D_2 - B_2) - G_2 + cu$					$+ ca$	$D_2 + G_2 - ca - cu$		B_2	$D_1 + B_1 + G_1 - cu$	E_1
Corporate 1	$(D_1 + B_1)$										$D_1 + B_1$
Corporate 2	$(D_1 + B_1)$										
Bank 1				$D_1 + B_1$						$D_1 + B_1$	$D_1 + B_1$
Bank 2					$D_2 + B_2$					$D_2 + B_2$	$D_2 + B_2$
CB 1	$G_1 + ca + cu$					$B_1 - G_1 - ca - cu$				B_1	B_1
CB 2	$G_2 - ca - cu$						$B_2 - G_2 + ca + cu$			B_2	B_2
Tot. Fin. Liabs				$D_1 + B_1$	$D_2 + B_2$	$B_1 + D_1$	$B_2 + D_2$	B_1	B_2		
Tot. Liabs		E_1	E_2	$D_1 + B_1$	$D_2 + B_2$	$B_1 + D_1$	$B_2 + D_2$	B_1	B_2		

Table 7.3 A balance of payment equilibrium within the corporate sectors of two countries

Corporate 1			
Real assets	$D_1 + B - X$	Loans Bank 1	$D_1 + B_1$
Claim to Corporate 2	$+ X$		
Corporate 2			
Real assets	$D_2 + B_2 + X$	Loans Bank 2	$D_2 + B_2$
		Liability to Corporate 1	$+ X$

by numerous emerging market crises (Mexico in the 1980s, Thailand, Indonesia and Russia in the late 1990s), and also in the euro area crisis.

Generally, observers may find current and capital accounts of specific countries in specific periods, as well as cumulated external positions of these countries, as something economically sensible and welfare improving, or as reflecting undesirable imbalances with the potential for financial destabilisation and corresponding welfare damage. For example, the large short-term foreign indebtedness of Germany that built up in the second half of the 1920s and that created the subsequent run on Germany in 1931 was assessed early as problematic (see e.g. annual reports of the Reichsbank in the 1920s). Similar cases were often observed until recently with emerging market economies. During his entire Presidency, US President Trump criticised German current account surpluses as unnatural and problematic, while the Bundesbank defended them as reflecting the German age pyramid and hence the need for the German society as a whole to save through the temporary accumulation of a net external claim.

Alternatives to settlement in gold
Returning now to the initial case in which the balance of payment is not balanced, i.e. $ca \neq -cu$, it should be noted that the resulting **net claim does not necessarily need to be settled through a physical gold transfer**, but it can also be settled through the creation of a foreign reserves claim of central bank 1 towards central bank 2. One could for example imagine that also under the gold standard, the two central banks have a settlement agreement in which cross border bank transfers are settled through a counterbalancing central bank position, up to a certain limit beyond which settlement in gold is required. This case is illustrated in the accounts in Table 7.4.

Table 7.5 shows still another alternative, namely that a claim of central bank 1 towards commercial bank 2 is created. For both central banks, this could make a difference: from the perspective of central bank 1, it could mean problems in case of a need to liquidate these claims when they are needed for interventions. For central bank 2, it could cause domestic financial stability issues, requiring it to act as LOLR to its domestic debtors when central bank 1 liquidates its foreign reserves for intervention purposes.

Returning to the base case that the international transactions are settled in gold and affect central bank gold reserves, two limits may eventually become binding:

Table 7.4 Central banks' accounts in gold standard with claims on gold instead of shipments

Central Bank 1			
Credit Bank	$B_1 - G_1 - ca - cu$	Banknotes	B_1
Gold reserves	G		
Gold Claim to CB 2	$+ ca + cu$		
Central Bank 2			
Credit Bank	$B_2 - G + ca + cu$	Banknotes issued	B_2
Gold reserves	G	Gold liability to CB $_1$	$+ ca + cu$

Table 7.5 Accounts of financial sectors if deposits with foreign banks replace gold shipment

Bank 1			
Loans corporate 1	$D_1 + B_1$	Deposits household 1	$D_1 + G_1 + cu$
		Deposits household 2	$+ ca$
		Credit central bank 1	$B_1 - G_1 - ca - cu$
Central Bank 1			
Credit Bank	$B_1 - G_1 - ca - cu$	Banknotes	B_1
Gold reserves	G		
Deposits Bank 2	$+ ca + cu$		
Bank 2			
Loans corporate 2	$D_2 + B_2$	Deposits household 2	$D_2 + G - ca - cu$
		Credit central bank 2	$B_2 - G$
		Deposit Central Bank 1	$+ ca + cu$
Central Bank 2			
Credit Bank 2	$B_2 - G$	Banknotes	B_2
Gold reserves	G		

first, the **limit with regard to the share of banknotes that needs to be covered by gold reserves,** according to the central bank law. For example, the Reichsbank was subject, according to its mandate established by the Dawes Plan in 1924, to a 40% gold coverage ratio for banknotes. Second, assuming that gold coverage ratios have been given up, when **gold reserves are fully exhausted,** such as in the case of the Reichsbank in July 1931. Then, eventually the gold convertibility has to be given up.

Performance of the gold standard

The gold standard worked fine during the period 1876–1914, but poorly in the interwar period. The poor interwar performance of the gold standard is explained by Eichengreen (1995) with the global scarcity of gold and non-collaborative international behaviour in the context of larger capital flow volatility due to the political and financial instabilities. The interwar gold standard came after the WWI experience that one cannot rely on a universal commitment of Governments to maintain a gold parity. For example, Germany devalued in 1924 by a factor of 10^9, and only very few like the US and the UK did not. Similarly, the belief in Governments to repay their debt was shaken (e.g. the Russian mega-default of 1917); moreover, the inter-war period was characterised by unsolved problems of international debt imbalances (war and reparation debt) and political instability, materialising in the rise of fascism and communism. Finally, the willingness of central banks to collaborate, e.g. through inter-central bank loans, was insufficient (while an international LOLR like the IMF was still missing). With increasing uncertainties after the outbreak of the global financial crisis in 1929, central banks were even keener to each hold sufficient gold reserves to be protected against future outflows, implying that on average central banks kept interest rates too high in their competition for the global gold stock, triggering deflation and depression.

7.2.2   The Bretton Woods System

The Bretton Woods system was set up in 1944 and included establishing the IMF and the World Bank. The related convertibility promises were given up in 1971 and 1974, although the role of the IMF as international LOLR has continued until today. The Bretton Woods system was a fixed exchange rate system in which the US committed to fix the value of the USD in gold (and to ensure convertibility), while the others promised to fix the price of their currency in USD (and to defend these fixed exchange rates). Therefore, in principle the US Fed needed gold as a reserve asset, while the other members needed USD. The accounts shown in Table 7.6 illustrates this situation, focusing on the case of flows handled through the foreign reserves of a non-US country. If country 2 is Germany, then in the Bretton Woods era (ca + cu) < 0, i.e. Germany had balance of payment surpluses and the Bundesbank accumulated foreign reserves.

Bordo (1993) notes that a fixed rate system of the **Bretton Woods type was subject to the following three problems**:

- **Adjustment**: "Under the classical gold standard, balance of payments adjustment worked automatically through the price specie flow mechanism, aided by short-term capital flows. .... Under Bretton Woods, concern over the unemployment consequences of wage rigidity delayed the deflationary adjustment required by a deficit country and, together with the use of short-term capital controls, considerably muted the automatic mechanism. .... The adjustment problem concerned the burden of adjustment between deficit and surplus countries and the choice of policy tools."
- **Liquidity**: "The perceived liquidity problem in the Bretton Woods system was that the various sources of liquidity were not adequate or reliable enough to finance the growth of output and trade. The world's monetary gold stock was insufficient by the late 1950s, IMF unconditional drawing rights were meagre, and the supply

Table 7.6 Two countries' financial accounts under the Bretton Woods system

Household 1			
Deposits Bank 1	$D_1 + G_1 + cu$	Household Equity	E_1
Banknotes	B_1		
Real Assets	$E_1 - D_1 - B_1 - G_1 - cu$		
Corporate 1 (USA)			
Real assets	$D_1 + B_1$	Loans Bank 1	$D_1 + B_1$
Bank 1 (USA)			
Loans corporate 1	$D_1 + B_1$	Deposits household 1	$D_1 + G_1 + cu$
Loans corporate 2	F	Deposits household 2	$D_{21} + ca$
		Credit central bank 1	$B_1 - G_1$
		Deposits Central Bank 2	$F - ca - cu$
Central Bank 1 (USA)			
Credit Bank 1	$B_1 - G_1$	Banknotes	B_1
Gold reserves	G_1		
Household 2			
Deposits Bank 2	$D_2 - ca - cu$	Household Equity	E_2
Deposits Bank 1	$D_{21} + ca$		
Banknotes	B_2		
Real Assets	$E_2 - D_2 - B_2 + cu$		
Corporate 2			
Real assets	$D_2 + B_2$	Loans Bank 2	$D_2 + B_2 - F$
		Loans Bank 1	**F**
Bank 2			
Loans corporate 2	$D_2 + B - F$	Deposits household 2	$D_2 - ca - cu$
		Credit central bank 2	$B_2 - F + ca + cu$
Central Bank 2			
Credit Bank	$B_2 - F + ca + cu$	Banknotes issued	B_2
Foreign reserves	$F - ca - cu$		

of U.S. dollars depended on the U.S. balance of payments, which in turn was related to the vagaries of government policy and the confidence problem."

- **Confidence**: "as in the interwar period, involved a portfolio shift between dollars and gold. As outstanding dollar liabilities held by the rest of the world monetary authorities increased relative to the U.S. monetary gold stock, the likelihood of a run on the "bank" increased. The probability of all dollar holders being able to convert their dollars into gold at the fixed price declined."

This led surplus countries to prefer hoarding gold instead of holding USD, i.e. a run on the US Fed's gold holdings took place by the surplus countries who made use of the US Fed's obligation to convert the surplus countries' USD into gold. Another way to describe the Bretton Woods problem is the **Triffin Dilemma** (Triffin 1960). In the words of the IMF (IMF 2020b):

> If the United States stopped running balance of payments deficits, the international community would lose its largest source of additions to reserves. The resulting shortage of liquidity could pull the world economy into a contractionary spiral, leading to instability. If U.S. deficits continued, a steady stream of dollars would continue to fuel world economic growth. However, excessive U.S. deficits (dollar glut) would erode confidence in the value of the U.S. dollar. Without confidence in the dollar, it would no longer be accepted as the world's reserve currency. The fixed exchange rate system could break down, leading to instability.

In principle, the solution of this problem was supposed to be the "SDR", the special drawing rights of the IMF, which created additional international liquidity.

Table 7.7 shows the case if the other country experiences balance of payment surpluses and the central banks prefer to accumulate gold instead of USD

The accounts in Table 7.6 had suggested that the US Fed's balance sheet was not really affected by the balance of payment deficits of the US—however this was not true, as highlighted by the Triffin Dilemma: Central bank 2 can also exchange its foreign reserves against gold, and this is indeed what central banks of balance of payment surplus countries tended to do. For example, the Bundesbank (until 1957 its predecessor, the Bank Deutscher Länder) had no gold reserves in 1949, but more than 3000 tons at the end of the Bretton Woods era in 1974. The desire to accumulate not only US dollars, but also gold, may have been understandable, since holding very large amounts of US dollars exposed a central bank to risks that the US eventually devalues—which it actually did. A bank run logic applies. The mechanics of the self-fulfilling prophecy works as follows in this case: if surplus countries start to doubt the ability or willingness of the US to defend the peg of the USD to gold, they are incentivized to start hoarding gold instead of USD, and eventually this leads the US to run out of gold reserves, forcing it to devalue the USD against gold, validating the fears of the countries who "ran" on the USD. Of course, at an early stage, the US could have tried to defend the peg by restrictive monetary policies which would have triggered capital inflows exceeding the negative effects of current accounts. But this would have had significant economic costs in the view of the responsible policy makers, and therefore did not take place. In the financial accounts, the tendency of surplus countries to hoard gold is reflected as follows, assuming the case that country 2 (Germany) has surpluses and converts these completely into gold (Table 7.7).

In retrospect, it appears that the Bretton Woods system could have worked if:

- balance of payment imbalances would have been limited;
- commitment of countries to defend the pegs had been very strong, even if this would require domestic adjustments. In view of its exposed role, the related commitment and credibility of the US was of overwhelming importance;
- the other countries accepted to mirror US monetary policies, including, for example, to import inflation, so as not to build up appreciation pressures, as e.g. the DM constantly did;

Table 7.7 Bretton Woods financial accounts if surplus countries hoard gold instead of USD

Bank 1 (USA)			
Loans corporate1	$D_1 + B_1$	Deposits household 1	$D_1 + G_1 - cu$
Loans corporate 2	FR	Deposits household 2	$D_{21} - ca$
		Credit central bank 1	$B_1 - G_1 + ca + cu$
		Deposits Central Bank 2	FR
Central Bank 1 (USA)			
Credit Bank	$B_1 - G_1 + ca + cu$	Banknotes issued	B_1
Gold	$G_1 - ca - cu$		
Bank 2 (Germany)			
Loans corporate 2	$D_2 + B_2 - FR$	Deposits household 2	$D + ca + cu_2$
		Credit central bank 2	$B_2 - FR - ca - cu$
Central Bank 2 (Germany)			
Credit Bank	$B_2 - FR - ca - cu$	Banknotes	B_2
Foreign reserves	FR		
Gold	$+ ca + cu$		

- the other countries accepted to accumulate USD as foreign exchange reserves, i.e. did not insist on accumulating gold, in case the US ran balance of payment deficits;
- an international LOLR (like the IMF) had given enough confidence to non-US countries about available liquidity in case of need, so that central banks would not have been tempted to build up excessively large foreign exchange reserves and thereby contribute to international imbalances.

There were several changes of pegs before the eventual dismissal of the Bretton Woods system in 1974.

7.3　International Monetary Frameworks of the Present

After the collapse of the Bretton Woods system in 1971, and its official dissolution with the Jamaica Accords of 1976, a "paper standard" emerged in which currencies were no longer pegged to gold. While the biggest economies opted for flexible, floating exchange rates, the smaller economies mostly fixed their exchange rate to that of the US or of the nearest large economy. The western European countries tried to develop arrangements for limiting the fluctuations of the currencies between each other, whereas the German Mark emerged as the anchor. Thereafter these agreements led to the creation of the euro.

7.3.1 Fixed Exchange Rate System—Paper Standard

The following financial accounts show a fixed exchange rate system in a paper standard. Country 1 is a large country, which does not care about the exchange rate, while country 2 is a smaller country that does care and that ensures that its currency is pegged 1:1. For example, country 1 could be the euro area and country 2 Bulgaria. To be able to defend the currency peg, the central bank of country 2 needs foreign reserves. In the accounts below, we assume that these have a level **FR** and are held in the form of deposits in currency 1 with Bank 1, and that they originated in the past from capital account inflows into country 2, which still materialize in the accounts in the form of lending of Bank 1 to corporate 2 of FR.

Table 7.8 illustrates the example of a **current account transaction in which a household in country 1 sells a car and exports it to a household in country 2**.

- Household 1 requires payment on its account at bank 1 and household 2 requests his Bank 2 to make an international payment to the account of household 1 at Bank 1.
- To do this, bank 2 needs deposits in country 1. If it has none, it will go to the foreign exchange (FX) market and offer deposits with itself, and demand deposits with some bank in country 1, so that it can then transfer funds to the account of household 1 in country 1.
- If the market was otherwise in equilibrium, this FX market transaction of bank 2 increases demand of currency 1 and supply of currency 2. This will bring the FX market into disequilibrium and push up the price of currency 1 measured in units of currency 2. Central bank 2 committed to a fixed exchange rate, and must therefore compensate the disequilibrium by increasing supply of currency 1 and demand of currency 2. It does this by selling deposits with bank 1 to bank 2 and debiting the current account of bank 2 with itself.
- Since bank 2 needs to restore zero deposits with central bank 2, it will increase its credit from central bank 2 by taking recourse to central bank 2 credit operations.

Exhausted central bank foreign reserves and the ILOLR

What if central bank 2's foreign reserves are exhausted, i.e. if $ca + cu > FR$? Eventually, the central bank and the government of country 2 have to restore macroeconomic conditions that stop and revert the flows that led to this situation (e.g. increase interest rates, strengthen the competitiveness through supply side reforms, etc.). However, such measures typically require some time to be effective. There are two short term options: either **Central bank 2 finds an** *international* **LOLR to replenish its foreign reserves**, or central bank 2 "defaults" on its promise to fix the exchange rate. In the latter case, the system moves towards a variable exchange rate system.

An international LOLR can take two forms: a direct lending between central banks, or through an intermediary like the IMF. Table 7.9 shows the latter case in a stylized way. **The intermediary (which we call "IMF") takes a loan from central**

Table 7.8 Two countries' financial accounts in paper standard with fixed exchange rates

Household 1			
Deposits Bank 1	$D_1 + cu$	Household Equity	E_1
Banknotes 1	B_1		
Real Assets	$E_1 - D_1 - B_1 - cu$		
Corporate 1			
Real assets	$D_1 + B_1$	Loans Bank 1	$D_1 + B_1$
Bank 1			
Loans corporate 1	$D_1 + B_1$	Deposits household 1	$D_1 + cu$
Loans corporate 2	FR	Deposits household 2	$+ ca$
		Credit central bank 1	B_1
		Deposits central bank 2	$FR - ca - cu$
Central Bank 1			
Credit Bank 1	$B_1 - G_1$	Banknotes 1	B_1
Household 2			
Deposits Bank 2	$D_2 - ca - cu$	Household Equity	E_2
Deposits Bank 1	$+ ca$		
Banknotes 2	B_2		
Real Assets	$E_2 - D_2 - B_2 + cu$		
Corporate 2			
Real assets	$D_2 + B_2$	Loans Bank$_2$	$D_2 + B_2 - FR$
		Loans Bank 1	FR
Bank 2			
Loans corporate 2	$D_2 + B_2 - FR$	Deposits household 2	$D_2 - ca - cu$
		Credit central bank 2	$B_2 - FR + ca + cu$
Central Bank 2			
Credit Bank	$B_2 - FR + ca + cu$	Banknotes 2	B_2
Deposits bank 1	$FR - ca - cu$		

bank 1 to obtain currency 1 and provides this as credit to central bank 2. The loan is assumed here to exactly close the gap of missing foreign reserves to stem the outflow due to current and capital account deficits.

The intermediary could also have initially, when founded as an international institution, created a sufficient balance sheet to accommodate such loans. This is displayed in Table 7.10, where the IMF balance sheet is initially based on paid-in capital. This paid in capital is "invested" by the IMF in the form of deposits with the central banks.

Table 7.9 Financial accounts, fixed exchange rate, with IMF providing additional foreign reserves obtained by credit line

Bank 1			
Loans corporate 1	$D_1 + B_1$	Deposits household 1	$D_1 + cu$
Loans corporate 2	FR	Deposits household 2	$+ ca$
		Credit CB_1	$B_1 - \max(0, -FR + ca + cu)$
		Deposits CB_2	$FR + \max(0, -FR + ca + cu)$

Central Bank 1			
Credit to banks	$B_1 - \max(0, -FR + ca + cu)$	Banknotes 1	B_1
Credit to IMF	$+ \max(0, -FR + ca + cu)$		

Bank 2			
Loans corporate 2	$D_2 + B_2 - FR$	Deposits household 2	$D_2 - ca - cu$
		Credit central bank 2	$B_2 - FR + ca + cu$

Central Bank 2			
Credit Bank 2	$B_2 - FR + ca + cu$	Banknotes 2	B_2
Deposits bank 1	$\max(0, FR - ca - cu)$	IMF Credit	$\max(0, -FR + ca + cu)$

IMF			
Credit to CB B	$\max(0, -FR + ca + cu)$	Credit from CB A	$\max(0, -FR + ca + cu)$

Table 7.10 Financial accounts, fixed exchange rate, with IMF providing additional foreign reserves obtained by pre-paid capital

Central Bank 1			
Credit to banks	$B_1 - \max(0, -FR + ca + cu)$	Banknotes 1	B_1
Paid-in Capital IMF	$IMFC/2$	IMF deposit	$IMFC/2 - \max(0, -FR + ca + cu)$

Central Bank 2			
Credit Bank 2	$B_2 - FR + ca + cu$	Banknotes 2	B_2
Paid-in Capital IMF	$IMFC/2$	IMF deposit	$IMFC/2$
Deposits bank 1	$\max(0, FR - ca - cu)$	IMF credit	$\max(0, -FR + ca + cu)$

IMF			
Deposit CB 1	$IMFC - \max(0, -FR + ca + cu)$	Paid-in capital	$IMFC$
Deposit CB 2	$IMFC$		
Credit to CB 2	$\max(0, -FR + ca + cu)$		

Devaluation and settlement of the implied negative central bank capital

A devaluation by a central bank under a fixed exchange rate system could in some sense be compared to a default of a commercial bank when it is no longer able to pay back deposits when these are withdrawn, as developed in Chap. 6. Based on this analogy, one could also aim at a model of runs on currencies, in which the no-run conditions would depend both on liquidity (quantity and liquidity of foreign exchange reserves of the central bank) and on "fundamentals" being the (maybe somewhat less obvious) analogue to solvency in the bank run model.

Table 7.11 Central bank accounts when currency 2 is devalued

Central Bank 1 (denominated in currency 1)			
Credit to banks	B_1	Banknotes 1	B_1
Central Bank 2 (denominated in currency 2)			
Credit Bank 2	$B_2 - FR$	Banknotes 2	B_2
Foreign reserves	0.5FR		
Negative equity	0.5FR		

Table 7.11 shows the case of an appreciation of currency 2. This is what happened to Germany during Bretton Woods (but it would be similar in a paper standard).

If currency 2 would depreciate, typically no profits (nor losses) occur for central bank 2 as this scenario most likely occurs when central bank 2 has exhausted its foreign reserves. If it had foreign currency reserves, then it would book a profit, or, if it were prudent and conservative, it would book instead revaluation reserves on its liability side. Returning to the case of an appreciation of currency 2: the accounts of country 1 are not affected, but the country 2 central bank books a loss and negative equity. If the Government of country 2 wants to repair this negative equity, then it may issue additional debt (or impose extra taxes on households) and recapitalize the central bank. At the end, the appreciation is at the expense of the wealth of household 2. One could say that the household 2 sold real assets to country 1, but was only paid for half of the value—retroactively because of the devaluation of currency 1 (USD).

7.3.2 Flexible Exchange Rate Systems

In Table 7.12, we denominate the accounts of country 1 in currency 1, and those of country 2 in currency 2, and introduce the exchange rate α, i.e. α units of currency 2 are worth one unit of currency 1. Now, **the central bank balance sheet is no longer available for counterbalancing private balance of payment flows**. Instead, the private market participants have to equilibrate the balance of payment on its own. Below, this takes place by letting banks create cross border claims and liabilities between each other, so that eventually the foreign exchange market is in equilibrium. Now call ca the capital account imbalance contributed by the household. The total capital account balance will be $ca + ca_B$, if we call ca_B the capital account contribution of the banking system. Necessarily, $ca + ca_B = cu$, i.e. the total capital account exactly balances the current account. This obviously implies that $ca_B = cu - ca$, i.e. the capital account contribution of the banking system will have to equal the difference between the current account imbalance and the capital account imbalance contributed by the households. If banks are less willing to provide some elasticity be entering cross-border exposures, then the adjustment of the exchange rate to imbalances of payment flows stemming from households will be more violent. In other words, the readiness of the financial system to look through short-term fluctuations of payment flows and to take temporarily cross border exposures is essential in this system to be relatively stable (in conjunction of course with adequate central bank and fiscal policies of the public authorities in both countries). If the private financial sector is only limitedly willing to provide elastic cross-currency liquidity services, this will imply more volatile foreign exchange rates, and possibly require a more activist central bank (through more frequent interest rate adjustments, or even sporadic foreign exchange interventions). This could also be a consequence of tight regulations of banks' risk taking, or a lack of economic capital of banks that makes them unwilling to take risks anyway. Bank 1 has accepted to export capital into country 2 by depositing foreign currency in bank 2, while bank 2 has accepted to import capital by getting indebted towards bank 1.

The net foreign position of the countries has evolved as it would have done under any other international monetary regime—according to the current account imbalance. **The net foreign position is also impacted by the exchange rate**. If the claim is denominated in currency 2, then a devaluation of currency 2 (i.e. an increase in α) implies that the net foreign position of country 1 (in currency 1) declines (while it did not change for country 2), etc. The central bank foreign reserves do not change, i.e. the central bank is neither involved in current account nor capital account flows.

7.3.3   The European Monetary Union

A monetary union like the euro area can be interpreted as a fixed exchange rate system in which the automatic creation of intra-central bank claims and liabilities plays the role of gold/foreign reserves/IMF loans in standard fixed exchange rate systems. The intra-central bank claims and liabilities are in the case of the euro area the so-called TARGET2 balances, which have found some attention starting in 2011 (e.g. Sinn and Wollmershäuser 2012; Bindseil and König 2012; Buiter and Rabhari 2012). The capital flow mechanics in the years up to 2012 are reviewed in more detail in Lane (2013). A recent comprehensive treatment is Hellwig (2019). The system of financial accounts in Table 7.13 assumes that country 1 has a balance of payment surplus and country 2 a balance of payment deficit. We assume that both current account and capital account imbalances originate from the household. The two households contribute to capital flight to the same extent by shifting bank deposits from country 2 to country 1. The payment matching the current account transaction is assumed to be from the account of household 2 with bank 2 to the account of household 1 with bank 1.

The Eurosystem consolidated balance sheet will look as follows is shown in Table 7.14.

Table 7.13 made a number of simplifications: for example, there are no cross-border loans of banks to corporates, and the Eurosystem does not invest into securities. These additional elements could be integrated of course.

Table 7.12 Two countries' accounts in a flexible exchange rate system

Household 1			
Deposits Bank 1	$D_1 + cu$	Household Equity	E_1
Banknotes	B_1		
Real Assets	$E_1 - D_1 - B_1 - cu$		
Corporate 1			
Real assets	$D_1 + B_1$	Loans Bank 1	$D_1 + B_1$
Bank 1			
Loans corporate 1	$D_1 + B_1$	Deposits household 1	$D_1 + cu$
Deposit Bank 2	$ca + cu$	Deposits household 2	$+ ca$
		Central bank credit	B_1
Central Bank 1			
Credit Bank	B_1	Banknotes 1	B_1
Household 2			
Deposits Bank 2	$D_2 - \alpha \cdot ca - \alpha \cdot cu$	Household Equity	E_2
Deposits Bank 1	$+ \alpha \cdot ca$		
Banknotes 2	B_2		
Real Assets	$E_2 - D_2 - B_2 + \alpha \cdot cu$		
Corporate 2			
Real assets	$D_2 + B_2$	Loans Bank 2	$D_2 + B_2$
Bank 2			
Loans corporate 2	$D_2 + B_2$	Deposits household 2	$D_2 - \alpha \cdot ca - \alpha \cdot cu$
		Deposit Bank 1	$+ \alpha \cdot ca + \alpha \cdot cu$
Central Bank 2			
Credit Bank	B_2	Banknotes issued	B_2

In contrast to foreign reserves, T2 balances are not limited. However, one constraint is the central bank collateral framework and to what extent banks can close the funding gap created by the Balance of Payment deficits through additional central bank credit. This is why Hans-Werner Sinn and other ECB critics have identified the **ECB collateral framework** as one key factors that allowed the Eurosystem to contribute to overcoming the balance of payment crisis associated with the sovereign debt crisis of 2009–2012. Once the cumulated Balance of Payment deficits exceed the initial level of banknotes circulating in country 1, the banking system would be in a liquidity surplus and the Eurosystem consolidated balance sheet would start to lengthen one-to-one with further surpluses of country 1.

Table 7.13 Two countries' accounts in the European Monetary Union exchange rate system

Household 1			
Deposits Bank 1	$D_1 + ca/2 + cu$	Household Equity	E_1
Deposits Bank 2	$D_{12} - ca/2$		
Banknotes	B_1		
Real Assets	$E_1 - D_1 - D_{12} - B_1 - cu$		
Corporate 1			
Real assets	$D_1 + D_{21} + B_1$	Loans Bank1	$D_1 + D_{21} + B_1$
Bank 1			
Loans corporate1	$D_1 + D_{21} + B_1$	Deposits Hh 1	$D_1 + cu + ca/2$
		Deposits Hh 2	$D_{21} + ca/2$
Deposits NCB 1	$Max(0, -(B_1 - ca - cu))$	Credit NCB 1	$Max(0, (B_1 - ca - cu))$
National Central Bank 1 (NCB1)			
Credit Bank 1	$Max(0, (B_1 - ca - cu))$	Banknotes issued	B_1
T2 claims	$Max(0, ca + cu)$	Deposits bank 1	$Max(0, -(B1 - ca - cu))$
		T2 liabilities	$Max(0, -(ca + cu))$
Household 2			
Deposits Bank 2	$D_2 - ca/2 - cu$	Household Equity	E_2
Deposits Bank 1	$D_{21} + ca/2$		
Banknotes	B_2		
Real Assets	$E_2 - D_2 - D_{21} - B_2 + cu$		
Corporate 2			
Real assets	$D_2 + B_2$	Loans Bank 2	$D_2 + B_2$
Bank 2			
Loans corporate 2	$D_2 + D_{12} + B_2$	Deposit household 2	$D_2 - ca/2 - cu$
		Deposit household 1	$D_{12} - ca/2$
Deposit NCB 2	$Max(0, -(B_2 + ca + cu))$	Credit NCB 2	$Max(0, B_2 + ca + cu)$
National Central Bank 2 (NCB2)			
Credit to bank 1	$Max(0, B2 + ca + cu)$	Banknotes	$B2$
T2 claims	$max(0, -(ca + cu))$	Deposits bank 2	$Max(0, -(B2 + ca + cu))$
		T2 liabilities	$Max(0, (ca + cu))$
ECB			
T2 claims	$ca + cu$	T2 liabilities	$ca + cu$

Table 7.14 Eurosystem consolidated balance sheet

Eurosystem			
Eurosystem credit	$B_1 + B_2 + max(0, -(B_1 - ca - cu)) + max(0, -(B_2 + ca + cu))$	Banknotes	$B_1 + B_2$
		Deposits of banks	$max(0, -(B_1 - ca - cu)) + max(0, -(B_2 + ca + cu))$

7.3.4 Foreign Reserves

Although in principle the time of universal fixed exchange rates ended in the 1970s, many central banks continue to manage their exchange rate by letting their foreign reserves fluctuate accordingly. From 2000 to 2013 foreign reserves increased in an unprecedented manner, with China overtaking Japan as the largest holder of official foreign reserves in 2005 and reaching in 2013 close to 4 trillion USD equivalent of foreign reserves. During the same period, the Eurosystem was also surpassed by a number of emerging economies. Switzerland is unique in terms of being a small advanced economy and nevertheless ranking third—reflecting its combat against appreciation in view of safe-haven flows in the context of the euro area sovereign debt crisis. How can one explain this rapid build-up of unprecedented foreign reserves in the years until 2014? IMF (2011, 9) reports the following most frequent answers to the question about the reasons for holding (high) reserves: 80%: "Buffer for liquidity needs"; 60%: "Smoothing of exchange rate volatility"; 30%: "Management of exchange rate level". One might speculate that the frequency of answers also reflect how potentially controversial different explanations are. In reality, the management of the exchange rate level, i.e. preventing appreciation, has likely been the most important reason for the very steep trend of reserve accumulation, which goes beyond needed liquidity buffers.

What do foreign reserves consist of?
As the IMF annual report for 2014 (appendix I, page 1) reveals, foreign reserves at the end of 2014 consisted to a very large extent of **foreign currency** (86%), while **gold** came second (10%) and **IMF related reserves** (including SDRs) were third (4%). The **currency composition of foreign reserves** at the end of 2013 was (according to the IMF annual report for 2014) dominated by USD holdings (66%), followed by the EUR (24%) and the GBP (6%). **In which form were the foreign exchange reserves held?** McCauley and Fung 2003 (see also Borio et al. 2008) report that in the year 2000, 75% were held in the form of securities, and 25% in the form of deposits with banks and money market instruments. The majority of deposits is offshore, i.e. not deposits in USD with US banks, but with banks located in other jurisdictions (mainly London, or other global foreign exchange centres).

Foreign reserves may be built-up in particular in four ways: (i) Accumulated balance of payment surpluses under a fixed exchange rate system (or managed float). (ii) Creation of mutual foreign reserves through a currency swap, possibly including the involvement of an international organisation like the IMF. This neither requires Balance of Payment surpluses, nor will it put pressure on the exchange rate. (iii) Obtaining the foreign claims without counter-flow through e.g. a war indemnity, or a grant. (iv) Acquiring reserves in the market without corresponding balance of payment surpluses, assuming variable exchange rates. Banks will, with some elasticity, finance this, i.e. will accept the corresponding capital account flows. However, the exchange rate of the country accumulating foreign reserves in this way will likely decline to some extent. Eventually balance of payment surpluses may then kick in as a consequence of the devaluation.

References

Abrahams, Michael, Tobias Adrian, Richard K. Crump, Emanuel Moench, and Yu. Rui. 2016. Decomposing Real and Nominal Yield Curves. *Journal of Monetary Economics* 84: 182–200.

Aglietta, Michel, and Benoît Mojon. 2014. Central Banking. In *The Oxford Handbook of Banking*, 2nd ed. Oxford: Oxford University Press.

Agostini, G, Juan P. Garcia, A. González, J. Jia, L. Muller, and A. Zaidi. 2016. Comparative Study of Central Bank Quantitative Easing Programs. *School of International and Public Affairs (SIPA), Columbia University.*

Ambler, Steve. 2009. Price-Level Targeting and Stabilisation Policy: A Survey. *Journal of Economic Surveys* 23 (5): 974–97.

Aristotle, Ernest Barker, and R. F. Stalley. 1998. *The Politics.* Oxford World's Classics. Oxford: Oxford University Press.

Armantier, Olivier, Eric Ghysels, Asani Sarkar, and Jeffrey Shrader. 2015. Discount Window Stigma During the 2007–2008 Financial Crisis. *Journal of Financial Economics* 118 (2): 317–35.

Armantier, Olivier, Helene Lee, and Asani Sarkar. 2015. History of Discount Window Stigma-Liberty Street Economics.

Auer, Raphael, Giulio Cornelli, and Jon Frost. 2020. Rise of the Central Bank Digital Currencies: Drivers, Approaches and Technologies. BIS Working Papers, No. 880, August.

Bagehot, Walter. 1873. *Lombard Street: A Description of the Money Market.* London: Henry S. King & Co.

Ball, Laurence M. 2014. The Case for a Long-Run Inflation Target of Four Percent. *IMF Working Paper* 14 (92).

Bech, Morten L, and Aytek Malkhozov. 2016. How Have Central Banks Implemented Negative Policy Rates? *BIS Quarterly Review*, March.

Beneš, Jaromír, and Michael Kumhof. 2012. The Chicago Plan Revisited. *IMF Working Paper* 12 (202).

Bindseil, Ulrich. 2004. The Operational Target of Monetary Policy and the Rise and Fall of Reserve Position Doctrine. ECB Working Paper Series, No. 372 (June): 46.

———. 2013. Central Bank Collateral, Asset Fire Sales, Regulation and Liquidity.

———. 2014. *Monetary Policy Operations and the Financial System.* Oxford University Press.

———. 2019. *Central Banking Before 1800: A Rehabilitation.* Oxford University Press, USA.

———. 2020. Tiered CBDC and the Financial System. ECB Working Paper Series No. 2351, January.

Bindseil, Ulrich, and Juliusz Jablecki. 2011. The Optimal Width of the Central Bank Standing Facilities Corridor and Banks' Day-to-Day Liquidity Management. ECB Working Paper Series, No. 1350, June.

© The Author(s) 2021

U. Bindseil and A. Fotia, *Introduction to Central Banking*,
SpringerBriefs in Quantitative Finance,
https://doi.org/10.1007/978-3-030-70884-9

————. 2013. Central Bank Liquidity Provision, Risk-Taking and Economic Efficiency. ECB Working Paper, No. 1542, May.

Bindseil, Ulrich, and Philipp Johann König. 2012. TARGET2 and the European Sovereign Debt Crisis. *Kredit Und Kapital* 45 (2): 135.

Bindseil, Ulrich, Clemens Domnick, and Jörg Zeuner. 2015. Critique of Accommodating Central Bank Policies and the "Expropriation of the Saver". ECB Occasional Paper, No. 161.

Bindseil, Ulrich, Marco Corsi, Benjamin Sahel, and Ad Visser. 2017. The Eurosystem Collateral Framework Explained. Occasional Paper Series, No. 189, May.

BIS, Bank for International Settlements. 2018. Financial Stability Implications of a Prolonged Period of Low Interest Rates, July.

————. 2019. *Unconventional Monetary Policy Tools: A Cross-Country Analysis. Report Prepared by a Working Group Chaired by Simon M Potter and Frank Smets.* CGFS Papers, No. 63. BIS.

————. 2020. Central Bank Digital Currencies: Foundational Principles and Core Features, October.

BIS Markets Committee. 2019a. Large Central Bank Balance Sheets and Market Functioning, October.

————. 2019b. Monetary Policy Frameworks and Central Bank Market Operations, October.

Blanchard, Olivier. 2017. *Macroeconomics* (Global Edition). Pearson.

BoE, Bank of England. 2020a. Bank of England Market Operations Guide: Our Tools. http://www.bankofengland.co.uk/markets/bank-of-england-market-operations-guide/our-tools.

————. 2020b. Central Bank Digital Currency: Opportunities, Challenges and Design. Discussion Paper, March, 57.

Boivin, Jean, Michael T. Kiley, and Frederic S. Mishkin. 2010. How Has the Monetary Transmission Mechanism Evolved Over Time? *Handbook of Monetary Economics* 3: 369–422.

BoJ, Bank of Japan. 2020a. Complementary Deposit Facility. https://www.boj.or.jp/en/mopo/measures/mkt_ope/oth_a/index.htm/.

————. 2020b. Complementary Lending Facility. https://www.boj.or.jp/en/mopo/measures/mkt_ope/len_a/index.htm/.

Bolton, Patrick, and Xavier Freixas. 2006. Corporate Finance and the Monetary Transmission Mechanism. *The Review of Financial Studies* 19 (3): 829–70.

Bordo, Michael D. 1993. The Bretton Woods International Monetary System: A Historical Overview. In *A Retrospective on the Bretton Woods System: Lessons for International Monetary Reform*, 3–108. University of Chicago Press.

Borio, Claudio, Gabriele Galati, and Alexandra Heath. 2008. FX Reserve Management: Trends and Challenges. BIS Papers.

Brancaccio, Emiliano, and Giuseppe Fontana. 2013. "Solvency Rule" Versus "Taylor Rule": An Alternative Interpretation of the Relation between Monetary Policy and the Economic Crisis. *Cambridge Journal of Economics* 37 (1): 17–33.

Brunnermeier, Markus K., and Yann Koby. 2019. The Reversal Interest Rate. NBER Working Paper Series 25406.

BuBa, Deutsche Bundesbank. 1976. *Deutsches Geld- und Bankwesen in Zahlen: 1876–1975.* Frankfurt am Main: Knapp.

————. 1995. *The Monetary Policy of the Bundesbank.*

Buiter, Willem H. 2009. Negative Nominal Interest Rates: Three Ways to Overcome the Zero Lower Bound. *The North American Journal of Economics and Finance* 20 (3): 213–38.

Buiter, Willem H, and Ebrahim Rahbari. 2012. The ECB as Lender of Last Resort for Sovereigns in the Euro Area.

Burda, Michael, and Charles Wyplosz. 2017. *Macroeconomics: A European Text*, 7th ed. Oxford and New York: Oxford University Press.

Cap, Adam, Mathias Drehmann, and Andreas Schrimpf. 2020. Monetary Policy Operating Frameworks: A Short Primer Based on a New Interactive Database. *BIS Quarterly Review*, December.

Clark, T.L. 1994. Nominal GDP Targeting Rules: Can They Stabilize the Economy? *Economic Review-Federal Reserve Bank of Kansas City* 79: 11–11.

Coase, Ronald H. 1937. The Nature of the Firm. *Economica* 4 (16): 386–405.

Cochrane, John H. 2011. Determinacy and Identification with Taylor Rules. *Journal of Political Economy* 119 (3): 565–615.

CPMI, Committee on Payment and Market Infrastructures, and Market Committee MC. 2018. Central Bank Digital Currencies. BIS Report, March.

D'Amico, Stefania, and Thomas B. King. 2011. Flow and Stock Effects of Large-Scale Treasury Purchases. *SSRN Electronic Journal.*

Davydenko, Sergei A., Ilya A. Strebulaev, and Xiaofei Zhao. 2012. A Market-Based Study of the Cost of Default. *The Review of Financial Studies* 25 (10): 2959–99.

Dewatripont, Mathias, and Eric Maskin. 1995. Credit and Efficiency in Centralized and Decentralized Economies. *The Review of Economic Studies* 62 (4): 541–55.

Diamond, Douglas W., and Philip H. Dybvig. 1983. Bank Runs, Deposit Insurance, and Liquidity. *Journal of Political Economy* 91 (3): 401–19.

Dobler, Marc, Simon Gray, Diarmuid Murphy, and Bozena Radzewicz-Bak. 2016. The Lender of Last Resort Function after the Global Financial Crisis. *IMF Working Papers* 16 (10).

Domanski, Dietrich, and Vladyslav Sushko. 2014. Rethinking the Lender of Last Resort: Workshop Summary. BIS Paper, No. 79a.

Dornbusch, Rudiger. 1976. Expectations and Exchange Rate Dynamics. *Journal of Political Economy* 84 (6): 1161–76.

Dötz, Niko, and Mark Andreas Weth. 2019. Redemptions and Asset Liquidations in Corporate Bond Funds. Discussion Paper, No. 11.

Dyson, Ben, and Graham Hodgson. 2016. Digital Cash: Why Central Banks Should Start Issuing Electronic Money. Positive Money.

EC, European Commission. 2011. European Union Accounting Rules.

ECB, European Central Bank. 2004. Risk Mitigation Methods in Eurosystem Credit Operations. *Monthly Bulletin May 2004*, May, 71–79.

———. 2013. ECB Further Reviews Its Risk Control Framework Allowing for a New Treatment of Asset-Backed Securities. European Central Bank, 18 July. https://www.ecb.europa.eu/press/pr/date/2013/html/pr130718.en.html.

———. 2015. The Financial Risk Management of the Eurosystem's Monetary Policy Operations, August, 52.

———. 2020a. Euro Area Bank Lending Survey (BLS). European Central Bank.

———. 2020b. Eurosystem Collateral Data. European Central Bank.

———. 2020c. Standing Facilities. European Central Bank.

———. 2020d. Survey on the Access to Finance of Enterprises (SAFE). European Central Bank.

———. 2020e. Report on a Digital Euro, October.

Eichengreen, Barry J. 1995. *Golden Fetters: The Gold Standard and the Great Depression, 1919–1939*. NBER Series on Long-Term Factors in Economic Development.

EU. 2007. *Treaty on the Functioning of the European Union. Treaty on the Functioning of the European Union.*

European Systemic Risk Board. 2016. *Macroprudential Policy Issues Arising from Low Interest Rates and Structural Changes in the EU Financial System: November 2016.* LU: Publications Office.

Ewerhart, Christian, and Jens Tapking. 2008. Repo Markets, Counterparty Risk, and the 2007/2008 Liquidity Crisis.

Fed, Federal Reserve System. 2020a. Federal Reserve Board—Term Deposit Facility. Board of Governors of the Federal Reserve System. https://www.federalreserve.gov/monetarypolicy/tdf.htm.

———. 2020b. Open Market Operations During 2019.

———. 2020c. Primary and Secondary Lending Programs.

———. 2020d. Speech by Chair Powell on New Economic Challenges and the Fed's Monetary Policy Review. Board of Governors of the Federal Reserve System, 27 August.

Flannery, Mark J. 1996. Financial Crises, Payment System Problems, and Discount Window Lending. *Journal of Money, Credit and Banking* 28 (4): 804–24.

Fleming, Michael J., and Asani Sarkar. 2014a. The Failure Resolution of Lehman Brothers. SSRN Scholarly Paper ID 2422433, Social Science Research Network, Rochester, NY.

———. 2014b. The Failure Resolution of Lehman Brothers. Liberty Street Economics, 3 April.

Friedman, Milton. 1982. Monetary Policy: Theory and Practice. *Journal of Money, Credit and Banking* 14 (1): 98–118.

Fudenberg, Drew, and Jean Tirole. 1991. Game Theory Mit Press. *Cambridge, MA*, 86.

Galí, Jordi. 2015. *Monetary Policy, Inflation, and the Business Cycle: An Introduction to the New Keynesian Framework and Its Applications*. Princeton University Press.

Glover, Brent. 2016. The Expected Cost of Default. *Journal of Financial Economics* 119 (2): 284–99.

Goldberg, Linda S., Craig Kennedy, and Jason Miu. 2010. Central Bank Dollar Swap Lines and Overseas Dollar Funding Costs. w15763. National Bureau of Economic Research.

Gonzalez, Fernando, and Phillipe Molitor. 2009. Risk Mitigation Measures and Credit Risk Assessment in Central Bank Policy Operations. In *Risk Management for Central Banks and Other Public Investors*, 303–39. Cambridge: Cambridge University Press.

Goodhart, Charles and Albert Eric. 1999. Myths About the Lender of Last Resort. *International Finance* 2 (3): 339–60.

Goodhart, Charles, and Gerhard Illing. 2002. *Financial Crises, Contagion, and the Lender of Last Resort: A Reader: A Reader*. Oxford: Oxford University Press.

Graeber, David. 2012. *Debt: The First 5000 Years*. Penguin UK.

Grasselli, Matheus R., and Alexander Lipton. 2019. The Broad Consequences of Narrow Banking. *International Journal of Theoretical and Applied Finance* 22 (01): 1950007.

Hamilton, James D. 1996. This Is What Happened to the Oil Price-Macroeconomy Relationship. *Journal of Monetary Economics* 38 (2): 215–20.

Heijdra, Ben J. 2017. *Foundations of Modern Macroeconomics*. Oxford University Press.

Hellwig, Martin. 2019. Target-Falle Oder Empörungsfalle?: Zur Deutschen Diskussion Über Die Europäische Währungsunion. *Perspektiven Der Wirtschaftspolitik* 19 (4): 345–82.

Holmstrom, Bengt, and Jean Tirole. 1997. Financial Intermediation, Loanable Funds, and the Real Sector. *The Quarterly Journal of Economics* 112 (3): 663–91.

Huang, Wenqian, and Előd Takáts. 2020. The CCP-Bank Nexus in the Time of Covid-19. Bank for International Settlements.

Huber, Joseph. 1999. Plain Money: A Proposal for Supplying the Nations with the Necessary Means in a Modern Monetary System.

Humphrey, Caroline. 1985. Barter and Economic Disintegration. *Man* 20 (1): 48–72.

IMF, International Monetary Fund, ed. 2009. *Balance of Payments and International Investment Position Manual*, 6th ed. Washington, DC: International Monetary Fund.

———, ed. 2014. *From Stabilization to Sustainable Growth*. Annual Report / International Monetary Fund 2014. Washington, DC.

———. 2020a. *Global Financial Stability Report, October 2020*. Washington: IMF.

———. 2020b. Money Matters, an IMF Exhibit—The Importance of Global Cooperation, System in Crisis (1959–1971), Part 4 of 7. https://www.imf.org/external/np/exr/center/mm/eng/mm_sc_03.htm.

Keister, Todd. 2016. Bailouts and Financial Fragility. *The Review of Economic Studies* 83 (2): 704–36.

Keister, Todd, and Daniel R Sanches. 2020. Should Central Banks Issue Digital Currency?

Kindleberger, Charles P. 1984. *A Financial History of Western Europe*. Routledge.

Kindleberger, Charles P., and Robert Z. Aliber. 2011. *Manias, Panics and Crashes: A History of Financial Crises*. Palgrave Macmillan.

KPMG. 2016. Money Issuance. Alternative Monetary Systems. A Report Commission by the Icelandic Prime Minister's Office, 44.

Kyle, Albert S. 1985. Continuous Auctions and Insider Trading. *Econometrica: Journal of the Econometric Society*, 1315–35.

Lane, Philip R. 2013. Capital Flows in the Euro Area. European Commission, Directorate-General for Economic and Financial Affairs. Economic Papers, No. 497.

Laubach, Thomas, and John C. Williams. 2003. Measuring the Natural Rate of Interest. *Review of Economics and Statistics* 85 (4): 1063–70.

———. 2016. Measuring the Natural Rate of Interest Redux. *Business Economics* 51 (2): 57–67.

Lavoie, Marc. 2014. *Post-Keynesian Economics: New Foundations*. Edward Elgar Publishing.

Law, John. 1705. *Money and Trade Considered, with a Proposal for Supplying the Nation with Money, 1705*. Augustus M. Kelley.

McCauley, Robert N, and Ben SC Fung. 2003. Choosing Instruments in Managing Dollar Foreign Exchange Reserves. *BIS Quarterly Review*, March.

Merton, Robert C. 1974. On the Pricing of Corporate Debt: The Risk Structure of Interest Rates. *The Journal of Finance* 29 (2): 449–70.

Niepelt, Dirk. 2020. Monetary Policy with Reserves and CBDC: Optimality, Equivalence, and Politics.

Nyborg, Kjell G. 2017. Central Bank Collateral Frameworks. *Journal of Banking & Finance* 76: 198–214.

Obstfeld, Maurice, and Kenneth Rogoff. 1995. The Mirage of Fixed Exchange Rates. *Journal of Economic Perspectives* 9 (4): 73–96.

Potter, Simon M, and Frank Smets. 2019. *Unconventional Monetary Policy Tools: A Cross-Country Analysis*.

Richter, Rudolf. 1989. *Money: Lectures on the Basis of General Equilibrium Theory and the Economics of Institutions*. Berlin Heidelberg: Springer-Verlag.

Riksbank, Sveriges Riksbank. 2020. *Economic Review 2, 2020*. 2020th ed. Economic Review 2. Sveriges Riksbank.

Rochet, Jean-Charles, and Xavier Vives. 2004. Coordination Failures and the Lender of Last Resort: Was Bagehot Right after All? *Journal of the European Economic Association* 2 (6): 1116–47.

Rogoff, Kenneth S. 2017. *The Curse of Cash: How Large-Denomination Bills Aid Crime and Tax Evasion and Constrain Monetary Policy*. Princeton University Press.

Schmitt-Grohé, Stephanie, and Martín Uribe. 2010. The Optimal Rate of Inflation. *Handbook of Monetary Economics* 3:653–722.

Sheets, Nathan, Edwin Truman, and Clay Lowery. 2018. The Federal Reserve's Swap Lines: Lender of Last Resort on a Global Scale. In *Conference Responding to the Global Financial Crisis: What We Did and Why We Did It, Hutchins Center, Brookings Institution* (11–12 September).

Sinn, Hans-Werner, and Timo Wollmershäuser. 2012. Target Loans, Current Account Balances and Capital Flows: The ECB's Rescue Facility. *International Tax and Public Finance* 19 (4): 468–508.

S&P, Standard & Poor's. 2020. 2019 Annual Global Corporate Default and Rating Transition Study.

Stiglitz, Joseph E., and Andrew Weiss. 1981. Credit Rationing in Markets with Imperfect Information. *The American Economic Review* 71 (3): 393–410.

Sylvestre, Julie, and Cristina Coutinho. 2020. The Use of the Eurosystem's Monetary Policy Instruments and Its Monetary Policy Implementation Framework Between the First Quarter of 2018 and the Fourth Quarter of 2019. ECB Occasional Paper, No. 2020245.

Thornton, Henry. 1802a. *An Enquiry into the Nature and Effects of the Paper Credit of Great Britain*. Routledge.

———. 1802b. *An Enquiry into the Nature and Effects of the Paper Credit of Great Britain* (with an Introduction by FA von Hayek). New York: Farrer & Rinehart.

Triffin, Robert. 1960. *Gold and the Dollar Crisis: The Future of Convertibility*. New Haven.

UN, United Nation, and European Commission EC. 2009. *System of National Accounts 2008*. UN.

Walsh, Carl E. 2017. *Monetary Theory and Policy*. MIT press.

Werner, Richard A. 2014. Can Banks Individually Create Money out of Nothing?—The Theories and the Empirical Evidence. *International Review of Financial Analysis* 36: 1–19.

———. 2016. A Lost Century in Economics: Three Theories of Banking and the Conclusive Evidence. *International Review of Financial Analysis* 46: 361–79.

Wicksell, Knut. 1898. *Geldzins Und Güterpreise: Eine Studie Über Die Den Tauschwert Des Geldes Bestimmenden Ursachen.* G. Fischer.

———. 1936. Interest and Prices: A Study of the Causes Regulating the Value of Money. London: Macmillan.

Williams, John C. 2016. Monetary Policy in a Low R-Star World. *FRBSF Economic Letter* 23: 1–23.

Williamson, Oliver Eaton. 1985. *The Economic Institutions of Capitalism: Firms, Markets, Relational Contracting.* New York: Free Press.

Woodford, Michael. 2003. *Interest and Prices: Foundations of a Theory of Monetary Policy.* Princeton, NJ and Woodstock, Oxfordshire [UK]: Princeton University Press.

Printed in Great Britain
by Amazon

18108481R00088